ACOUSTIC ROCK GUITAR BASICS

Learn to play the guitar chords, solos, and riffs that rock masters like Neil Young, Dave Matthews, James Taylor, and more use in their biggest hits.

By Andrew DuBrock

Publisher: David A. Lusterman
Group Publisher and Editorial Director: Dan Gabel
Education Editor: Dan Apczynski
Director of Design and Production: Barbara Summer
Production Manager: Hugh O'Connor
Print Production: Emily Fisher

Cover Photograph: Barbara Summer

© 2012 Stringletter

ISBN 978-1-978-1-936604-19-7

This book was produced by Stringletter, Inc.
PO Box 767, San Anselmo, CA 94979-0767
(415) 485-6946; Stringletter.com

Library of Congress Cataloging-in-Publication Data

DuBrock, Andrew.
  Acoustic rock basics : learn to play the guitar chords, solos, and riffs that rock masters like
Neil Young, Dave Matthews, James Taylor, and more use in their biggest hits / by Andrew
DuBrock.
    p. cm. -- (Acoustic guitar private lessons)
  Includes bibliographical references.
  ISBN 197-8193660419
  1. Guitar--Methods (Rock)--Self-instruction. 2. Rock music--Instruction and study. I. Title.
  MT588.D83 2011
  787.87'193166--dc23
                        2011035543

Contents

Introduction 5

Notation Guide 6

ROCK CHORDS

Sus and Add Chords 10

Learn how artists like the Eagles and Tom Petty add texture and movement to songs by using "sus" and "add" chords, simple embellishments to chords you already know.

Slash Chords 17

Add bass notes to common chord shapes to create moving bass lines and capture the classic sounds of Cat Stevens and Eric Clapton.

Open-String Chords 22

Learn how classic bands use movable chord shapes to maximize the use of open strings in song accompaniment.

Creating Chordal Riffs 29

Learn how artists like Neil Young and the Beatles created classic riffs by deconstructing simple chord shapes and progressions.

SONG ACCOMPANIMENT

Alternating-Bass Fingerpicking 34

Learn to play versatile rhythm and accompaniment by training your picking thumb and fingers to work independently.

Single-Note Riffs and Backup 39

Learn how to back up your songs by playing unique single-note lines instead of strumming full chords.

Percussive Rhythm Techniques 43

Use scratch rhythms, picking-hand tapping, and percussive slapping to add energy to your rhythm guitar playing.

Alternate Tunings in Acoustic Rock 50

Learn how bands like Led Zeppelin and Fleetwood Mac adapted alternate tunings from folk and blues styles.

Expand Your Fingerpicking Accompaniment 56

Add variation to your song accompaniment by including fills, bass runs, and pauses in common fingerpicking patterns.

SOLOING AND PLAYING LEAD

Soloing with Pentatonic Scales 62

Give your scales a bluesy sound by using the minor-pentatonic scale, or a southern-rock sound by using the major-pentatonic scale.

Play Leads with Major and Minor Scales 68

Western music's two most popular scales provide a foundation for all your lead lines and solos.

Play Leads with Arpeggios 75

Open up your lead playing with easy, movable arpeggios that work with any chord progression.

About the Author 82

Audio

The complete set of audio tracks for the musical examples and songs in *Acoustic Rock Basics* is available for free download at **AcousticGuitar.com/ARBAudio**. Just add the tracks to your shopping cart and enter the discount code "**ARBTracks12**" during checkout to activate your free download.

1   Introduction and Tune-Up

Sus and Add Chords
2   Example 1
3   Example 2
4   Example 3–4
5   Example 5–6
6   Example 7
7   Example 8
8   Example 9
9   Headin' for the Freeway (Played with a full band, then played without the band)

Slash Chords
10   Example 1–2
11   Example 3–4
12   Example 5–6
13   Headin' for the Freeway (Played with a full band, then played without the band)

Open String Chords
14   Example 1–2
15   Example 3–4
16   Example 5
17   Example 6–7
18   Example 8–9
19   Example 10
20   Example 11
21   Virginia (Played with a full band, then played without the band)

Creating Chordal Riffs
22   Example 1
23   Example 2–4
24   Example 5
25   Example 6–7
26   Example 8
27   Example 9–10
28   Example 11–13
29   Taken by the Law

Alternating-Bass Fingerpicking
30   Example 1–2
31   Example 3–5
32   Example 6–7
33   Example 8–9
34   Example 10–11
35   Example 12–13
36   Example 14–17
37   The Troubadour

Single-Note Riffs and Backup
38   Example 1–2
39   Example 3–4
40   Example 5
41   Example 6–10
42   Example 11–14
43   Example 15–16
44   Sunlight

Percussive Rhythm Techniques
45   Example 1–2
46   Example 3
47   Example 4–5

48   Example 6
49   Example 7–8
50   Example 9
51   Example 10
52   Right About You

Alternate Tunings in Acoustic Rock
53   Dropped D Tuning
54   Example 1
55   Example 2
56   Example 3–4
57   Example 5–6
58   D A D G A D Tuning & Example 7
59   Open G Tuning & Example 8
60   C A C G C E Tuning
61   Llanfair (song)

Expand Your Fingerpicking Accompaniment
62   Example 1–2
63   Example 3–4
64   Example 5–6
65   Example 7–8
66   Example 9
67   Example 10–13
68   Break of Day (Played with a full band, then played without the band)

Soloing with Pentatonic Scales
69   Example 1–2
70   Example 3–5
71   Solo Blue
72   Example 6–7
73   Example 8–9
74   Example 10–11
75   Sky-Blue Solo

Play Leads with Major and Minor Scales
76   Example 1–2
77   Example 3
78   Example 4
79   Example 5–6
80   Example 7–8
81   Example 9
82   Sunnyside Solo
83   Example 10–11
84   Example 12
85   Example 13
86   Example 14–15
87   Example 16
88   Example 17
89   Full Moon Solo

Play Leads with Arpeggios
90   Example 1–3
91   Example 4–5
92   Example 6
93   Example 7
94   Example 8
95   Example 9
96   Example 10
97   Example 11–12
98   Example 13–14
99   Arpeggio Annie (Played with a full band, then played without the band)

Introduction

The acoustic guitar has always been one of the pillars of rock, passing from the hands of influential folk and blues players to the rock 'n' roll stars that followed in their footsteps. In the '50s, rock pioneers like Elvis and Buddy Holly used acoustic guitars to craft and perform many of the songs that helped shape the entire rock genre—"Blue Suede Shoes," "Heartbreak Hotel," "Peggy Sue," and "Well All Right," among others. British invasion bands like the Beatles and the Rolling Stones crafted catchy licks and propulsive rhythms on steel-string guitar, thickening the sound with a 12-string or creating a ringing backdrop with open tunings. Other classic rock and pop icons like Crosby, Stills, Nash and Young; the Eagles; Simon and Garfunkel; and James Taylor made acoustic guitar an integral part of '60s and '70s rock. Even supercharged rockers like Led Zeppelin, Eric Clapton, the Who, and the Allman Brothers Band put down their electrics to emulate and pay homage to the more organic sounds of their blues, folk, and Celtic heroes—whether it was thumping, foot-stomping acoustic blues, droning alternate tunings, or upbeat southern-rock strumming. And as the 20th century rolled on, modern acts like Tom Petty, the Dave Matthews Band, and Jack Johnson kept their acoustics front and center, able to make their single-note melodies and acoustic licks heard over the din of electric instruments thanks to major advances in live sound engineering and equipment.

In *Acoustic Rock Basics*, we'll study techniques from all of these artists and more and learn how they used their acoustic guitars within a rock or pop context. The book is divided into three sections, starting with a group of lessons on chords. In these lessons, we'll study the types of chords bands like the Eagles, Eric Clapton, and Tom Petty used in their classic hits, and we'll see how acts like the Beatles and Neil Young crafted riff-based songs around chords.

The song accompaniment section explores alternate tunings, percussive techniques like scratch rhythm, picking patterns like alternate bass fingerpicking, and more advanced fingerpicking techniques that highlight free-flowing melodies and allow for accompaniment without pattern picking. The book finishes with a section on lead playing and investigates how classic rock acts used pentatonic scales, major and minor scales, and arpeggios to craft leads and anthemic instrumental melodies and hooks.

It's all here in *Acoustic Rock Basics*. So sit down, grab your trusty acoustic guitar, and dive in. Whether you want to connect with rock's primal roots by hacking out full-bodied chords or connect with its ethereal evolution by plucking out precise single-note licks, there's a technique or tool to help everyone rock!

—*Andrew DuBrock*

Introduction and Tune-Up TRACK 1

Notation Guide

Reading music is no different than reading a book. In both cases, you need to understand the language that you're reading; you can't read Chinese characters if you don't understand them, and you can't read music if you don't understand the written symbols behind music notation.

Guitarists use several types of notation, including standard notation, tablature, and chord grids. Standard notation is the main notation system common to all instruments and styles in Western music. Knowing standard notation will allow you to share and play music with almost any other instrument. Tablature is a notation system exclusively for stringed instruments with frets—like guitar and mandolin—that shows you what strings and frets to play at any given moment. Chord grids use a graphic representation of the fretboard to show chord shapes for fretted stringed instruments. Here's a primer on how to read these types of notation.

Standard Notation

Standard notation is written on a five-line staff. Notes are written in alphabetical order from A to G. Every time you pass a G note, the sequence of notes repeats—starting with A.

The duration of a note is determined by three things: the note head, stem, and flag. A whole note (○) equals four beats. A half note (♩) is half of that: two beats. A quarter note (♩) equals one beat, an eighth note (♪) equals half of one beat, and a 16th note (♬) is a quarter beat (there are four 16th notes per beat).

The fraction (4/4, 3/4, 6/8, etc.) or **c** character shown at the beginning of a piece of music denotes the time signature. The top number tells you how many beats are in each measure, and the bottom number indicates the rhythmic value of each beat (4 equals a quarter note, 8 equals an eighth note, 16 equals a 16th note, and 2 equals a half note).

The most common time signature is 4/4, which signifies four quarter notes per measure and is sometimes designated with the symbol **c** (for common time). The symbol **¢** stands for cut time (2/2). Most songs are either in 4/4 or 3/4.

Tablature

In tablature, the six horizontal lines represent the six strings of the guitar, with the first string on the top and sixth on the bottom. The numbers refer to fret numbers on a given string.

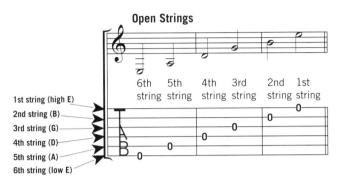

The notation and tablature in this book are designed to be used in tandem—refer to the notation to get the rhythmic information and note durations, and refer to the tablature to get the exact locations of the notes on the guitar fingerboard.

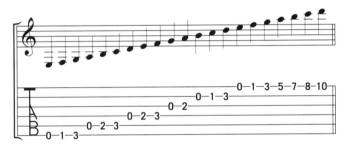

Fingerings

Fingerings are indicated with small numbers and letters in the notation. Fretting-hand fingering is indicated with 1 for the index finger, 2 the middle, 3 the ring, 4 the pinky, and *T* the thumb. Picking-hand fingering is indicated by *i* for the index finger, *m* the middle, *a* the ring, *c* the pinky, and *p* the thumb. Circled numbers indicate the string the note is played on. Remember that the fingerings indicated are only suggestions; if you find a different way that works better for you, use it.

Strumming and Picking

In music played with a flatpick, downstrokes (toward the floor) and upstrokes (toward the ceiling) are shown as follows. Slashes in the notation and tablature indicate a strum through the previously played chord.

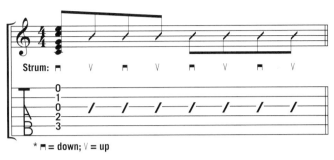

* ⊓ = **down**; ∨ = **up**

In music played with the pick-hand fingers, *split stems* are often used to highlight the division between thumb and fingers. With split stems, notes played by the thumb have stems pointing down, while notes played by the fingers have stems pointing up. If split stems are not used, pick-hand fingerings are usually present. Here is the same fingerpicking pattern shown with and without split stems.

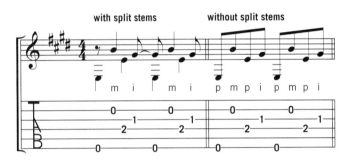

Chord Diagrams

Chord diagrams show where the fingers go on the fingerboard. Frets are shown horizontally. The thick top line represents the nut. A fret number to the right of a diagram indicates a chord played higher up the neck (in this case the top horizontal line is thin). Strings are shown as vertical lines. The line on the far left represents the sixth (lowest) string, and the line on the far right represents the first (highest) string. Dots show where the fingers go, and thick horizontal lines indicate barres. Numbers above the diagram are left-hand finger numbers, as used in standard notation.

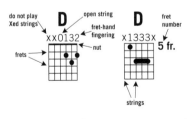

Again, the fingerings are only suggestions. An *X* indicates a string that should be muted or not played; 0 indicates an open string.

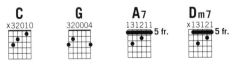

Capos

If a capo is used, a Roman numeral indicates the fret where the capo should be placed. The standard notation and tablature is written as if the capo were the nut of the guitar. For instance, a tune capoed anywhere up the neck and played using key-of-G chord shapes and fingerings will be written in the key of G. Likewise, open strings held down by the capo are written as open strings.

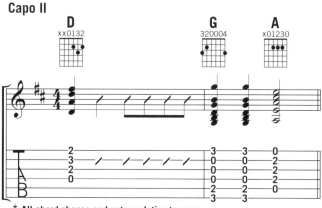

* All chord shapes and notes relative to capo

Tunings

Alternate guitar tunings are given from the lowest (sixth) string to the highest (first) string. For instance, D A D G B E indicates standard tuning with the bottom string dropped to D. Standard notation for songs in alternate tunings always reflects the actual pitches of the notes. Arrows underneath tuning notes indicate strings that are altered from standard tuning and whether they are tuned up or down.

Tuning: D A D G B E

Vocal Tunes

Vocal tunes are sometimes written with a fully tabbed-out introduction and a vocal melody with chord diagrams for the rest of the piece. The tab intro is usually your indication of which strum or fingerpicking pattern to use in the rest of the piece. The melody with lyrics underneath is the melody sung by the vocalist. Occasionally, smaller notes are written with the melody to indicate other instruments or the harmony part sung by another vocalist. These are not to be confused with cue notes, which are small notes that indicate melodies that vary when a section is repeated. Listen to a recording of the piece to get a feel for the guitar accompaniment and to hear the singing if you aren't skilled at reading vocal melodies.

You've got to move

Articulations

There are a number of ways you can articulate a note on the guitar. Notes connected with slurs (not to be confused with ties) in the tablature or standard notation are articulated with either a hammer-on, pull-off, or slide. Lower notes slurred to higher notes are played as hammer-ons; higher notes slurred to lower notes are played as pull-offs. While it's usually obvious that slurred notes are played as hammer-ons or pull-offs, an H or P is included above the tablature as an extra reminder.

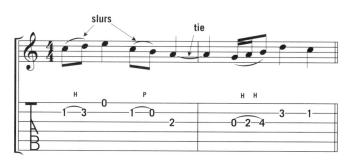

Slides are represented with a dash, and an S is included above the tab. A dash preceding a note represents a slide into the note from an indefinite point in the direction of the slide; a dash following a note indicates a slide off of the note to an indefinite point in the direction of the slide. For two slurred notes connected with a slide, you should pick the first note and then slide into the second.

Bends are represented with upward curves, as shown in the next example. Most bends have a specific destination pitch—the number above the bend symbol shows how much the bend raises the string's pitch: 1/4 for a slight bend, 1/2 for a half step, 1 for a whole step.

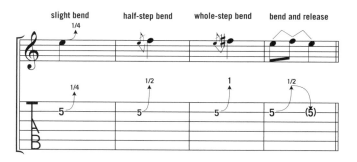

Grace notes are represented by small notes with a dash through the stem in standard notation and with small numbers in the tab. A grace note is a very quick ornament leading into a note, most commonly executed as a hammer-on, pull-off, or slide. In the first example below, pluck the note at the fifth fret on the beat, then quickly hammer onto the seventh fret. The second example is executed as a quick pull-off from the second fret to the open string. In the third example, both notes at the fifth fret are played simultaneously (even though it appears that the fifth fret, fourth string, is to be played by itself), then the seventh fret, fourth string, is quickly hammered.

Harmonics

Harmonics are represented by diamond-shaped notes in the standard notation and a small dot next to the tablature numbers. Natural harmonics are indicated with the text "Harmonics" or "Harm." above the tablature. Harmonics articulated with the right hand (often called artificial harmonics) include the text "R.H. Harmonics" or "R.H. Harm." above the tab. Right-hand harmonics are executed by lightly touching the harmonic node (usually 12 frets above the open string or fretted note) with the right-hand index finger and plucking the string with the thumb or ring finger or pick. For extended phrases played with right-hand harmonics, the fretted notes are shown in the tab along with instructions to touch the harmonics 12 frets above the notes.

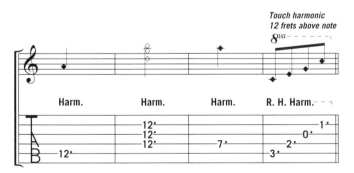

Repeats

One of the most confusing parts of a musical score can be the navigation symbols, such as repeats, *D.S. al Coda*, *D.C. al Fine*, *To Coda*, etc. Repeat symbols are placed at the beginning and end of the passage to be repeated.

You should ignore repeat symbols with the dots on the right side the first time you encounter them; when you come to a repeat symbol with dots on the left side, jump back to the previous repeat symbol facing the opposite direction (if there is no previous symbol, go to the beginning of the piece). The next time you come to the repeat symbol, ignore it and keep going unless it includes instructions such as "Repeat three times."

A section will often have a different ending after each repeat. The example below includes a first and a second ending. Play until you hit the repeat symbol, jump back to the previous repeat symbol and play until you reach the bracketed first ending, skip the measures under the bracket and jump immediately to the second ending, and then continue.

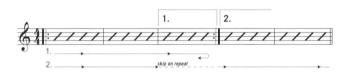

D.S. stands for *dal segno* or "from the sign." When you encounter this indication, jump immediately to the sign (𝄋). *D.S.* is usually accompanied by *al Fine* or *al Coda*. Fine indicates the end of a piece. A coda is a final passage near the end of a piece and is indicated with ⊕. *D.S. al Coda* simply tells you to jump back to the sign and continue on until you are instructed to jump to the coda, indicated with *To Coda* ⊕.

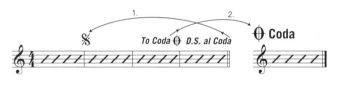

D.C. stands for *da capo* or "from the beginning." Jump to the top of the piece when you encounter this indication.

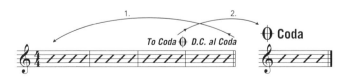

D.C. al Fine tells you to jump to the beginning of a tune and continue until you encounter the *Fine* indicating the end of the piece (ignore the *Fine* the first time through).

Sus and Add Chords

An acoustic rock hit often hooks you with a unique-sounding chord or the way one chord leads perfectly into the next. Many popular songs accomplish this magic with first-position root chords very similar to those that you probably already know, but with slight variations that bring them alive and add a new flavor to common chord progressions. Artists like the Eagles and Tom Petty have crafted hit after hit using these altered chord types, called "sus" and "add" chords. Most of these are fairly easy to learn, and they open up new possibilities for simple but interesting chord progressions, so let's dive in and take a look at each type.

Sus Chords

The major and minor chords you already know are made up of three notes—the root (or first note in the corresponding scale), third, and fifth. The third of a chord is what gives major and minor chords their character. The major third in a major chord gives it that distinctive "happy" sound, while the minor third in a minor chord gives it a distinctive "sad" sound.

A *sus* (or "suspended") chord substitutes another note for that all-important third. The lack of the third's distinctive sound means that sus chords can be played with or substituted for either major or minor chords. (See "Building Sus and Add Chords" on page 11 for more about the theory behind these chords and how to build them.) We'll look at three of the most common types of sus chords in this lesson: the sus4, 7sus4, and sus2.

Sus4 Chords

Sus4 chords (the "4" refers to the note that is substituted for the third in these chords) are the most common sus chords, heard in countless classic songs and often played as part of a progression with their major or minor counterparts. Let's see what these chords sound like by comparing an E and an Esus4 chord. To play the Esus4, start with an E chord and lay your pinky down on the second fret of the third string, one fret above where your index finger is when playing the E chord.

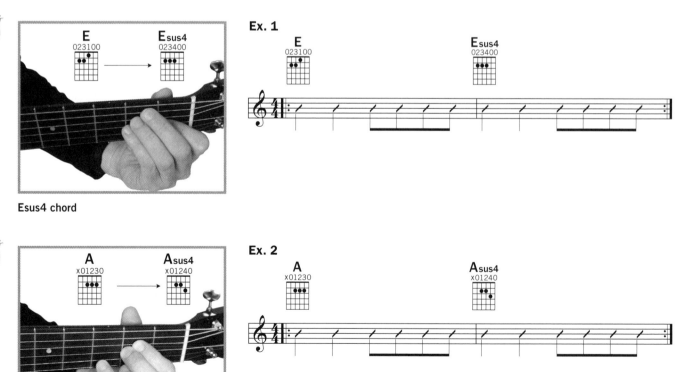

Esus4 chord

Asus4 chord

The "sus4" part of this chord is the note you're playing with your pinky, and it's replacing the note your index finger plays in an E chord—the third. Shifting between these two chords already gives you a great-sounding effect (**Example 1**). This chord change is similar to the one used in the opening of the Eagles' "Peaceful Easy Feeling."

Now let's look at an Asus4 chord. For this one, start with an A chord, then add your pinky to the third fret of the second string, as shown in the photo on page 10.

Example 2 re-creates a sound similar to the "Peaceful Easy Feeling" opening using A chords.

For a Dsus4 chord, start with a D chord and add your pinky on the third fret of the first string, as in the photo, right. Think about the signature progression in Tom Petty's "Free Fallin'" for an immediate example of the power of the sus4! (Though you'll need to put a capo on the third fret to sound like Petty does on record.)

So far we've alternated between major chords and their sus4 counterparts to help you identify the telltale sus4 sound,

but you can also play sus4 chords on their own, in place of major chords within a chord progression. **Example 3** shows a chord progression reminiscent of the opening to "Take It Easy," another Eagles classic. Notice how the C chord calls for you to leave your pinky holding down the G note on the third fret of the high E string. This makes for a smooth transition from the C chord to the Dsus4 chord, since both of those chords have that very note, and you can leave your pinky parked on the third fret for the whole progression. While a D chord would work fine in this context, the Dsus4 adds an interesting open sound that you just don't get with a stock D.

Seventh chords also sound great as sus4 chords. In fact, the single A7sus4 in **Example 4** sounds an awful lot like the intro to "A Hard Day's Night" by the Beatles.

See "More Sus Chords" on page 12 for more examples of easy sus4 and 7sus4 chords.

Ex. 3

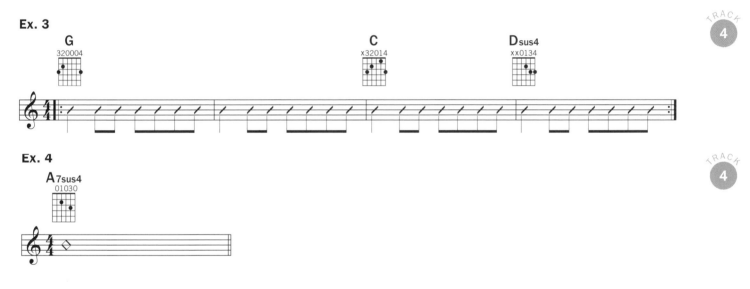

Ex. 4

Building Sus and Add Chords

Major and minor scales are both built from their own set of seven distinctive notes (for more on major- and minor-scale construction, see the Play Leads with Major and Minor Scales lesson on page 68). Each of these scale degrees are labeled root through seventh, in order. When you move from the seventh back to the root again, that root can also be called the eighth degree, and each consecutive step afterwards is one degree higher. For instance, the ninth is the same note as the second, but it's up an octave (the distance of one cycle through the scale).

Once you know these degrees you can create any sus or add chord. If you want to build a sus4 chord, simply add the fourth degree and leave out the third. If you want to build an add4 chord, just add that fourth to a major chord.

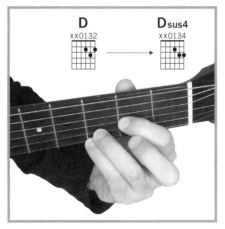

Dsus4 chord

Sus2 Chords

Sus2 chords are the next most commonly heard sus chords. The "2" refers to the second degree of a chord's scale—the note that is substituted for the third in a sus2 chord. To play an Asus2 chord, start with an A chord and lift your ring finger off of the second string (see photo).

Example 5 uses both Asus2 and Asus4 chords, so that you can hear the difference between the two types. As we've already seen, both of these chords replace the third in a chord with another note. So far, we've only used major chords, but to see how this sounds with minor chords, try **Example 6**.

Add9 Chords

Add chords are similar to sus chords, but with one major difference. With a sus chord you substitute a note for another note, but in an add chord, you *add* a note to that chord. Add chords sound thicker than sus chords, because they have more notes; they also sound major or minor, because they include that distinctive third degree. While there are a few different notes you can add to a chord, the most common note to add is the ninth, which creates an add9 chord, and we'll explore that type in this lesson.

The easiest add9 chord to grab is Cadd9. From a C chord, add your pinky to the third fret of the second string to get this chord, shown on page 13.

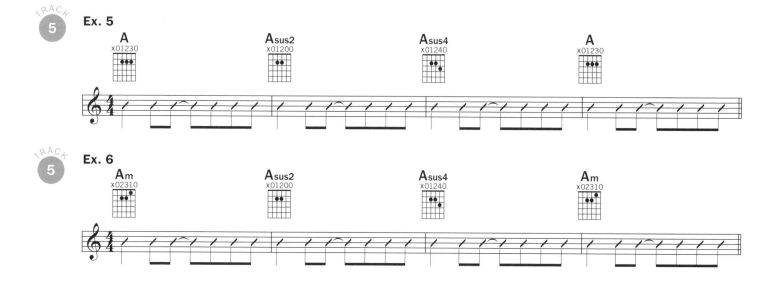

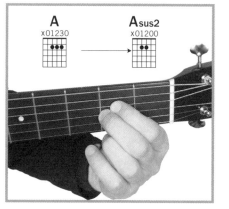

Asus2 chord

More Sus Chords

Here are some other common sus2, sus4, and 7sus4 chords at the nut of your guitar.

Add9 chords have a fuller sound than their major or minor counterparts, and you can hear it in **Example 7**'s G–D–Cadd9 chord progression. Think about the riff in Third Eye Blind's "Semi-Charmed Life" or the opening to Green Day's "(Good Riddance) Time of Your Life," both of which make use of add9 chords.

The Gadd9 chord is easy enough to grab. Simply move your middle finger from the fifth string up to the third string. Make sure to dampen the fifth string by rolling your ring finger down and lightly touching it, as shown in the lower right-hand photo.

Example 8 shows the Gadd9 chord in action. In this context, it alternates with a standard G chord to add some interest to several measures of G—adding contrast and giving the impression that things are moving forward. Gordon Lightfoot fingerpicks a similar chord change with a capo on fret two in one of his biggest hits, "If You Could Read My Mind."

Eadd9 and Aadd9 chords are a bit more difficult to play. In both of these chords, you have to stretch your pinky over two frets. But the extra difficulty has a substantial payoff, which you'll hear when you play these huge-sounding chords shown on page 14.

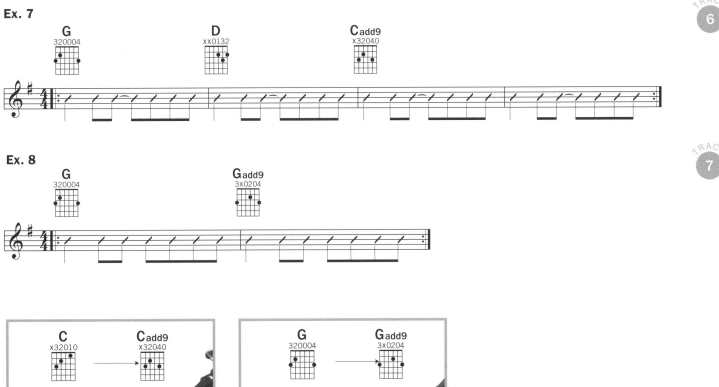

Ex. 7

TRACK 6

Ex. 8

TRACK 7

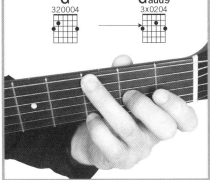

Cadd9 chord   Gadd9 chord

Chords like these bring the arpeggiated intro to the Police's "Every Breath You Take" to life. Imagine how that song would sound with stock major chords.

To compare the sounds in a different context, **Example 9** uses the lush Eadd9 chord to enhance the classic D–A–E chord progression, substituting the Eadd9 for a standard E chord. Then compare this sound with the generic E-chord version to see how it changes the sound by adding extra color in the middle of the chord—having that add9 note so close to the third above it (on the G string) creates a much lusher sound than duplicating a third E note would (as a standard E chord does).

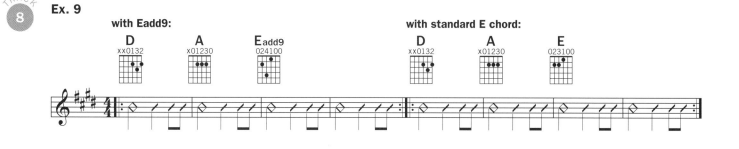

Ex. 9

TRACK 8

with Eadd9:

D
xx0132

A
x01230

E add9
024100

with standard E chord:

D
xx0132

A
x01230

E
023100

A add9
x01420

Aadd9 chord

E add9
024100

Eadd9 chord

More Add Chords

Here are some other common add chords at the nut of your guitar.

F add9
xx3214

E add9
023104

C add4
x34010

E m(add9)
013000

A m(add9)
x02410

F m(add9)
xx3114

Headin' for the Freeway

Words and music by Andrew DuBrock

Now let's try using these types of chords in a song! "Headin' for the Freeway" uses several suspended chords based on moves the Eagles use throughout their repertoire. Notice how the Dsus2 chord in measure 11 creates a melody line on the top string that starts with the open string, moves up to the second fret for the D chord in the next measure, and finishes on the third fret for the G chord. The Eagles use the Dsus4–D progression, as you see in measures 27–28, to facilitate their signature soaring vocal harmony. The Dsus4 in measure 32 is played as a whole note, and the pause punctuates the end of the chorus with the open-ended sound we explored in Example 3. Once you've got this tune under your fingers, try finding places for these new chords within your own songs.

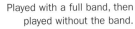 Played with a full band, then
played without the band.

 TRACK 9

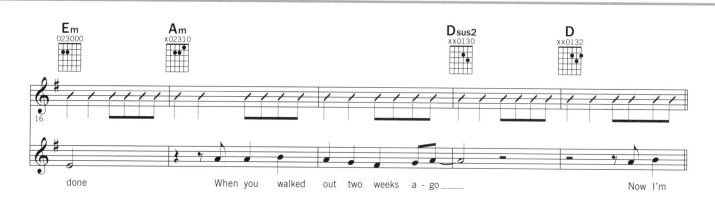

done   When you walked out two weeks a - go_____   Now I'm

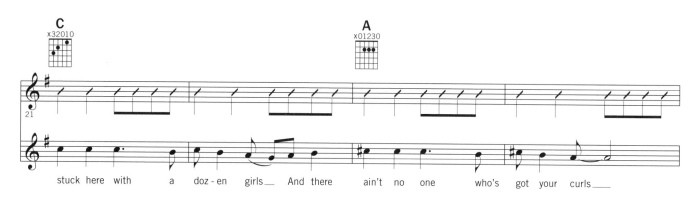

stuck here with   a   doz - en girls_ And there   ain't no one   who's got your curls_____

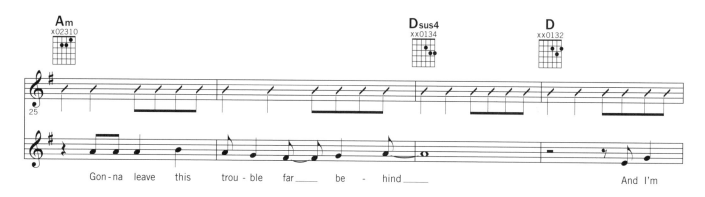

Gon - na leave this   trou - ble far_____ be - hind_____   And I'm

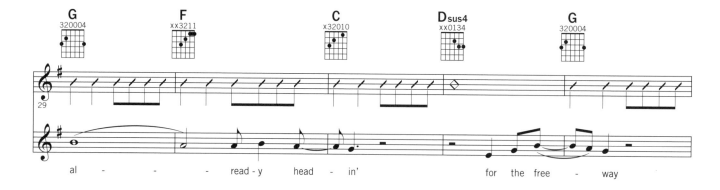

al - - - read - y head - in'   for the free - way

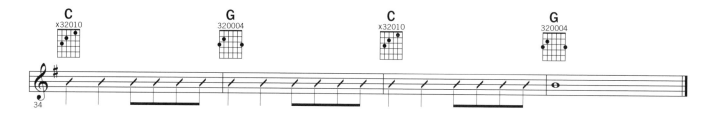

Slash Chords

In the Sus and Add Chords lesson, you learned how to incorporate sus and add chords into your repertoire, expanding your root-position backup options substantially. But there are even more colors you can explore with standard chords down at the nut of your guitar. Think about the opening chords to Cat Stevens's "Father and Son" or the Rolling Stones' "You Can't Always Get What You Want." Both of these songs get their distinctive character by using "slash chords," which have bass notes different from standard minor and major chords and can be effective in creating moving bass lines and transitions between chords. In this lesson, you'll learn how to form several common slash chords and use them in progressions as well as in an entire song.

Slash chords get their name from the slash that appears within each chord's label. When reading a slash chord, the chord is to the left of the slash and the bass note is to the right. For example, the G/B chord is a G-major chord with a B note in the bass and is called "G over B."

Slash chords often work well as transition chords. **Example 1** shows how the G/B chord works seamlessly between C and Am chords. This sounds similar to Bob Marley's "Redemption Song."

D/F♯ is another common slash chord. There are a number of ways to play this chord, but the easiest version uses your index finger on the sixth string. Playing the open fifth string in this chord tends to make the sound muddy, so roll your fretting-hand index finger down to damp the fifth string. While you *can* play a D/F♯ with a full D chord on top, it's easier to use this three-finger version that omits the highest string. You could also use your thumb to fret the lowest string.

This chord works well between G and Em chords, as shown in **Example 2**. Eric Clapton's "Tears in Heaven" has a similar progression (though Clapton plays his tune in a different key, which we'll touch on in a minute).

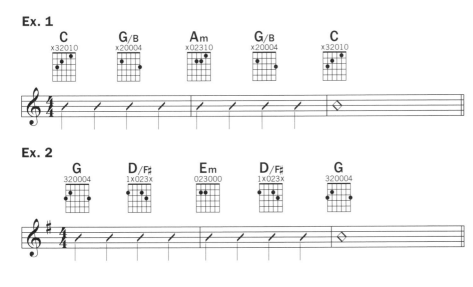

Ex. 1

Ex. 2

G/B chord   D/F♯ chord

E/G♯ is another slash chord that can be a little tricky to grab. Use your ring finger on the sixth string and roll it down to damp the fifth string.

I like how this chord transitions between A and G, especially in the Asus2–E/G♯–G–D progression shown in **Example 3**. Notice how the motion from the Asus2 to the E/G♯ chord sounds similar to the C–G/B progression in Example 1. They are essentially the same chord change played in different keys. This key (A) is where Clapton plays his "Tears in Heaven" progression. If you start with an A chord, play the E/G♯, and end on an F♯m chord, you'll hear it.

Sometimes you can add the same bass note to different voicings of a standard chord, opening up unique possibilities. For instance, you can play a C/G chord two ways, and each works better in different contexts.

The first voicing works great as a thick-sounding C chord that you can use in place of any C chord. The second version (below, far right), however, works really well as an embellishment to a G chord. Make sure you damp the fifth string with your ring finger when you play this version. **Example 4** shows this C/G chord in a progression similar to the beginning of the chorus of the Eagles song "Lyin' Eyes." This is also the chord Cat Stevens alternates with a G chord in the opening of "Father and Son."

So far, we've created slash chords by using bass notes of open-position chords that are part of the standard chord but not

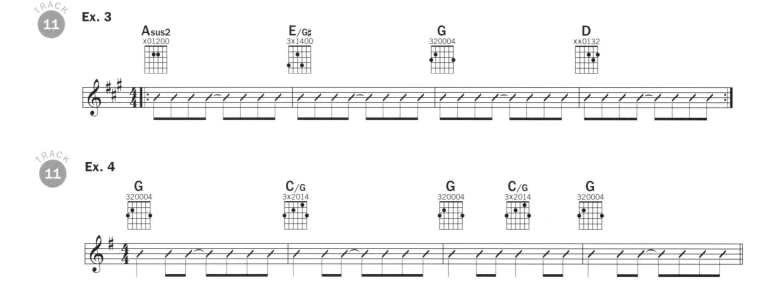

E/G♯ chord

C/G chord

C/G chord

the typical "root" bass note. For instance, the G note in a C/G chord *is* part of a C chord. But some slash chords have bass notes that *aren't* part of the basic chord. Below you'll find a couple examples of these chord types (the C/D, D/C, and F/G chords).

These chords come in handy in many places. While a D/C chord might sound a little muddy if played by itself, it works great when moving from D to other chords, as in the moving bass line in **Example 5.** (Note that while the C note is not part of the standard D major chord, it does technically turn the D into another common chord, a D7.)

And the F/G chord works well when moving from a G to a C chord. All of these are common in popular songs, and the Eagles even use the F/G chord near the end of the chorus in "Lyin' Eyes" in a progression similar to **Example 6**. Make sure you damp the fifth and first strings of the F/G and pay attention to the fingering—this is one of the more difficult root-position chords to finger.

In these first two lessons, we've explored several ways to make standard major and minor chords more interesting. Take it easy on the number of sus, add, and slash chords you use. Too many will make the chords stick out, but a few well-placed chords will add variety and a sense of movement to your songs.

C/D Chord

D/C Chord

F/G Chord

Headin' for the Freeway

Words and music by Andrew DuBrock

Now let's integrate some slash chords into my song "Headin' for the Freeway" (from the Sus and Add Chords lesson) to emulate more moves that the Eagles use in their songs. First, let's change the intro so that you rock between G and C/G chords, as in Example 4, adding some movement to the beginning of the tune and contrast to the G–C chord change that kicks off the verse. I've also added an F/G chord at the end of the chorus, injecting a bit of the "Lyin' Eyes" sound we experimented with in Example 6.

Played with a full band,
then played without the band.

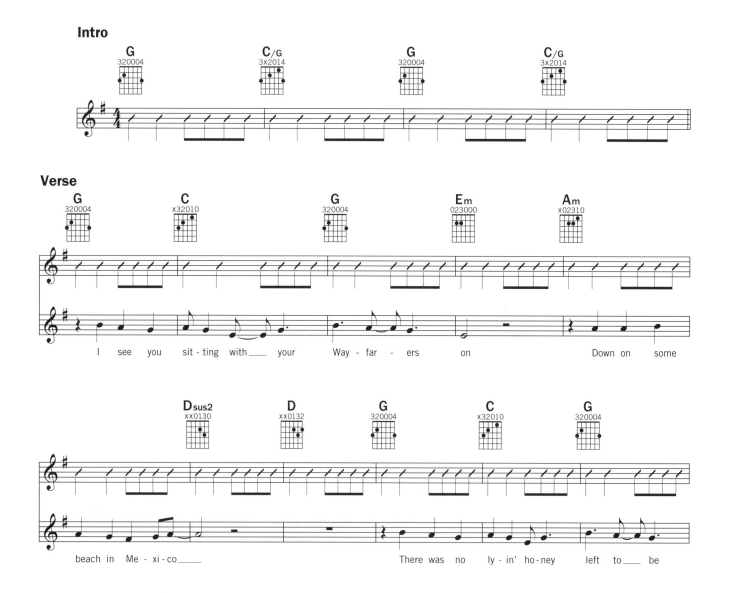

done   When you walked out two weeks a - go_____   Now I'm

stuck here with   a doz - en girls_____ And there   ain't no one   who's got your curls_____

Gon - na leave this   trou - ble far_____ be - hind_____   And I'm

al - - - read - y head - in'   for the free - way

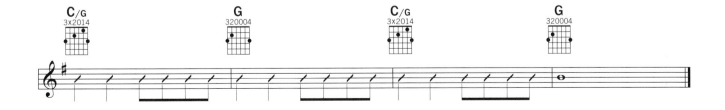

Open String Chords

You may have wondered how pop-rock icons like John Mayer, the Beatles, or the Allman Brothers write songs with huge-sounding chords that don't sound like typical root-position shapes. Listen closely and you'll often hear ringing open strings—like the high open E and B strings from a standard E chord—but *these* chords sound much more exciting than that plain E chord. Fortunately, these artists aren't using knuckle-busting chord shapes or obscure alternate tunings. Instead, they're moving basic three- and four-finger chord shapes around the fretboard—just like you do with barre chords—but including open strings to fill out the chord with additional tones while also enhancing the chord's sustain. In this lesson, we'll explore these open-string sounds, giving you the

tools to create your own songs the same way that the Allman Brothers, the Beatles, or John Mayer have. You'll also have the ability to enhance familiar old tunes by plugging open-string shapes in place of their standard-chord counterparts.

Slide Shapes Up the Fretboard

The quickest way to create lush open-string chords is to take a familiar root-position chord shape and slide it up the fretboard, finding other spots where it sounds good. Let's try this with a D chord shape. **Example 1** shows places where this shape works well. As the shape moves up, so does the chord name, but the open D-string bass note stays the same. That's why these chords

are labeled as *slash* chords. (In slash chords, the basic chord is on the left of the slash and the bass note is on the right. See the complete Slash Chords lesson on page 17.) But we're less concerned with chord names than sounds, and this shape sounds great as you slide it up the fretboard. The intro and outro to the Beatles' "Eight Days a Week" uses a line very similar to **Example 2**.

Now let's try this with another first-position chord shape—E (**Example 3**). Using these shapes, we can play something similar to Example 2, this time in the key of E (**Example 4**). An A shape will also work, and don't forget minor chords. As you hear in **Example 5**, the Dm shape works well and other minor shapes will, too, particularly Em and Am.

Modify Shapes for More Flexibility

You can also move open-string chords with fretted bass notes around, although some of the chords you find will sound better if you modify them a bit. Let's slide a C shape up the fretboard to illustrate this (**Example 6**). Notice that the bass note of each

of these chords changes, instead of staying the same, as in the previous examples. That's the main difference with this chord shape.

The Fmaj9 chord sounds OK, but it's a little thick for what I'm looking for, so I modified it by adding another note from the C shape (**Example 7**). If you visualize the complete C shape (including the open first and third strings), you'll see where the third-string, fifth-fret note in the Fmaj7 chord in Example 7 comes from. But you'll have to rearrange your fingers to fret this chord. Grab the original C shape with your pinky, ring, and middle fingers on the fifth, fourth, and second strings, respectively. This leaves your index finger free to fret the added note on the third string. Make sure none of your fretting-hand fingers flatten out to touch the open first string—you want the E note to ring through (otherwise it wouldn't be an open-string chord anymore!). You can try this idea of adding fretted notes from the basic chord with other open-string chords that sound discordant.

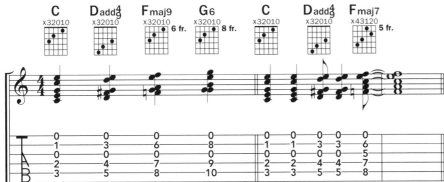

Keep your fingers arched when playing the Fmaj7 chord in Example 7.

Add Root Bass Notes

Notice that Examples 1–5 used slash chords, but Examples 6 and 7 don't. That's because the bass note is fingered in the first-position C chord, so it slides up with the rest of the shape, instead of being an open-string drone in the D, E, and A shapes. While the chords in Examples 1–5 sound huge, they don't highlight chord changes as strongly in a progression as chords where the bass note is the root. You can easily make those slash chords sound more like the chord to the left of the slash by adding root bass notes to the open-string shapes, taking advantage of the proximity of the root notes as you move up the neck. For example, if you add bass notes to the E-shape chords in Example 3, you get the chords in **Example 8**, all of which have a root note on the sixth string and will more clearly define a chord change. Now check

out how these chords change the sound of the progression from Example 2 (**Example 9**).

Notice that the chords in Examples 8 and 9 are essentially barre-chord shapes with the barre removed (flatten your index finger across all the strings for the familiar barre-chord shape). **Example 10** shows how you can find similar open-string sounds with a minor barre-chord shape (F#m) and a seventh-chord shape (F#7). Notice that in the minor shape (labeled F#m11) the sixth string is fretted with your thumb on the second fret, which can be a challenge! Also note that in the seventh-chord shape (labeled F#11) the fifth string is muted, making it easier to grab. Often, you'll have to mute a string in a movable chord instead of trying to fret it in its original shape.

Fret the sixth string with your thumb when playing the F#m11 chord in Example 10.

Create Your Own Chords

You can apply these concepts to any chord you can imagine. A basic rule of thumb is that if an open string is a note that fits within the major or minor scale affiliated with the key you're in, it should work. If it's not in the key, you may have to play a fretted note on that string. But this is just a general rule, and it's often good to experiment *before* you rule any combinations out. For instance, the F#11 chord in Example 9 has an A# note in it, which doesn't match the underlying E-major scale of that example; instead, it functions as the #11th in the key of E, but it still sounds great. Of course, if a shape *doesn't* sound good when you move it to a different place, try modifying it. If a shape doesn't have any open strings, find a way to include open strings, then move it around the fretboard. John Mayer applied all these concepts in his hit song "Daughters," which features a chord progression similar to **Example 11**.

Now let's try playing a complete song using movable open-string shapes. "Virginia" has an open-string pattern that is similar to the progression in the Allman Brothers' classic "Melissa." It starts with open-string shapes moved up the fretboard over static bass notes, as in the chords in Examples 1–5. Notice that the G#m/E and F#m/E chords are Em shapes slid up the fretboard, while the D/E chord in measure 3 uses three notes of a C shape up two frets. In measure 12, the initial chord-shape pattern switches to an A/E chord (the E-shape chord moved up the fretboard) before shifting gears by adding root bass notes to the shapes in the next section (measures 13–22). Here, E- and Em-shape chords and A- and Am-shape chords create a propulsive chord progression before returning to the opening progression in measure 23.

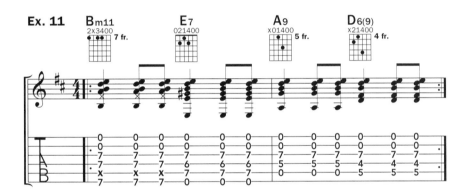

Virginia

Words and music by Andrew DuBrock

TRACK
21

Played with a full band,
then played without the band.

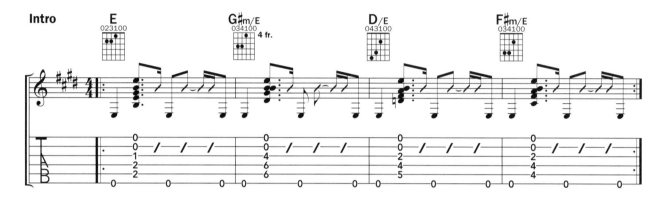

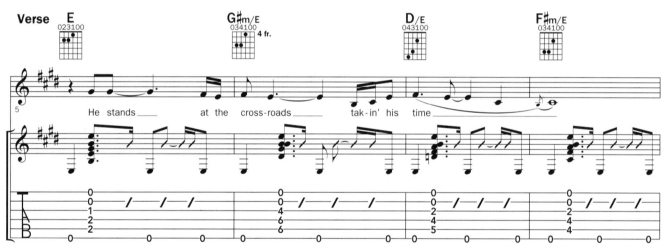

He stands_____ at the cross-roads_____ tak-in' his time_____

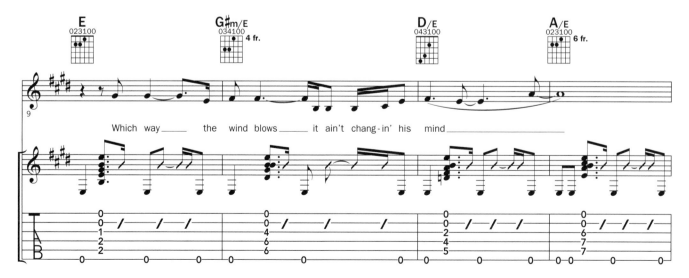

Which way_____ the wind blows_____ it ain't chang-in' his mind_____

Back to Vir - gin - ia _____

Creating Chordal Riffs

When you first hear a catchy lick or riff, it may sound so good that you expect it to be a difficult lead technique requiring hours of practice to master. That's a natural conclusion to jump to, since we're often shown images of lead guitarists quickly navigating their fretboards with blurred fingers. But many of the best licks and riffs by artists like the Beatles and Neil Young are really just made up of bits and pieces of easy chord shapes. In this lesson, you'll learn how to apply a few tricks to these shapes and the way you put them together, so you can come up with your own ear-catching riffs.

Deconstruct Chord Shapes

When you look at a simple D chord, you may not see all the potential within that three-fingered shape, but you can find countless great riffs within this chord—the Beatles crafted the instantly recognizable lines to "Norwegian Wood" and "Here Comes the Sun" based on the first-position D chord. Keep this shape rooted in your mind while you explore **Example 1**, which first shows a D chord, and then shows shapes you can access from

this position by moving around just one finger at a time. Many of these shapes have slightly different names—for instance, the first one to the right of the D chord is a Dsus4 (as explained in the Sus and Add Chords lesson). But we're not worried about the names here; we're more interested in how we can create interesting-sounding parts by embellishing a chord shape. Strum through each one and practice switching between them.

Once your fingers are comfortable with the shapes, you can use them to create melodies. **Example 2** shows a melody to start with, focusing on single notes. The key to now making **Example 3** sound like this melody instead of a bunch of chords is to highlight those melody notes from Example 2 as you play through the riff. Notice how you're strumming through four strings in the first and second measures, but in the third and fourth measures, only two or three strings are strummed—that's because the melody notes are focused on the second and third strings in the later measures, so strumming through the whole chord (especially the higher notes on the higher strings) at those points would obstruct the melody.

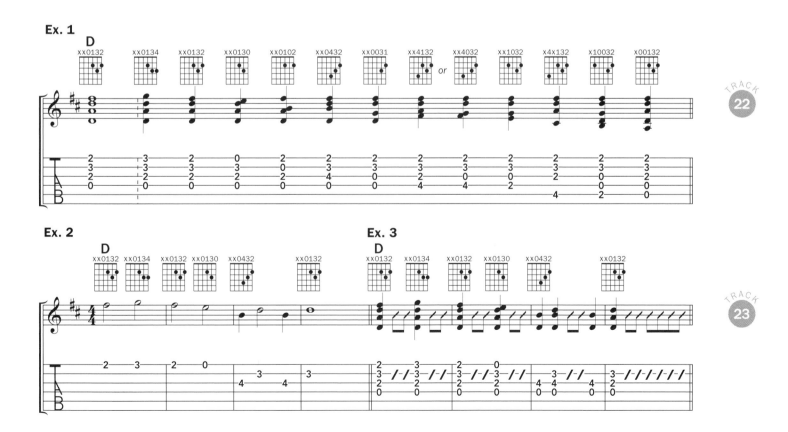

Don't worry about hitting *precisely* the strings shown in the notation every time—this can really hang up your ability to play through the riff. It's much more important to focus on what the melody notes are, and when you do that, you'll often bring them out naturally. If you hit the melody note and a string above it instead of the string below it, it will probably still sound fine. The point is: don't get so bogged down in the details that you lose the feel of the riff.

One way to get a better feel for the melody is to separate it completely from the chord strums, as in **Example 4**. You may even prefer it this way. With melody notes on the lower strings, I often use single-note runs like this or incorporate dyads (two notes), as in Example 3 (in the third measure).

Once you get the hang of creating melodies like this, you can add even more variation by moving other chord shapes into the mix. **Example 5** adds Cadd9 and G/B chord shapes to a D-shape melody to create a riff similar to the Beatles' "Norwegian Wood."

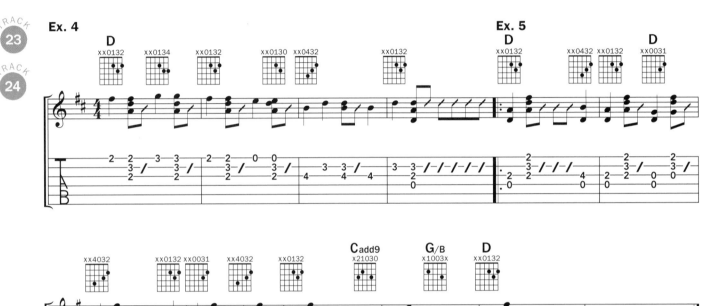

Turn Progressions into Riffs

You can also create chordal riffs by starting with a chord progression and picking out individual notes or partial chords. With a little experimentation, you can find a cool pattern in most any chord progression. Take, for instance, the simple A–Asus2 chord progression in **Example 6**. By picking out individual notes of each chord, you come up with the riff in **Example 7**—something similar to the Beatles' "Ticket to Ride."

Example 7 is fairly short, but riff-like chord progressions often fuse together a few pieces to create a longer guitar break or verse backup to a song. Let's try this by starting with the four-

measure progression in **Example 8**. Apply a picking pattern to highlight some of the chord changes, and we end up with the riff-like progression in **Example 9**, which sounds similar to the beginning of Neil Young's "Needle and the Damage Done." Picking out these individual notes sounds nice, but it can also be fairly difficult to master—especially on a long progression like this. If it's troublesome, don't worry too much about picking each string individually. Instead, shoot for a grouping of strings around your target, like in **Example 10**. You'll get a similar effect with a little less difficulty, and if it's easier for you to keep the groove going, it's going to sound better.

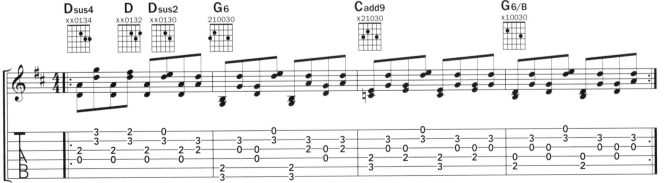

Next, let's add to this progression. **Example 11** shows another four-measure progression that we can tack onto the four measures from Examples 9 and 10 to create a complete guitar break or verse backup. Since we've been picking out a fairly steady pattern for the first four measures, let's try something different in **Example 12** by adding hammer-ons in the first and third beats of the first measure (notated with a "H") and a walk down over our Fmaj7 chord—essentially dressing up the Fmaj7 chord by embellishing it

with one-finger moves like we tried in examples 1–5. To play the hammer-ons, pluck the open third string, then hammer your middle finger down onto the third string at the second fret with enough force to sound the note. For the final measures (**Example 13**), you'll go back to picking out the individual notes of the chords, playing quarter notes to keep the flow steady from the previous two measures.

TRACK 28

Ex. 11

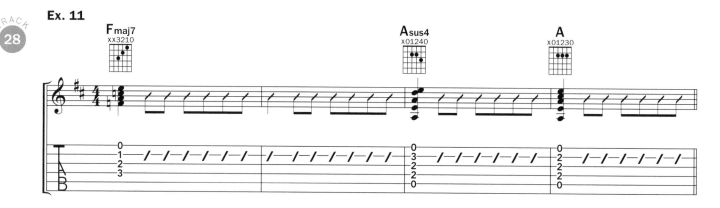

TRACK 28

Ex. 12   **Ex. 13**

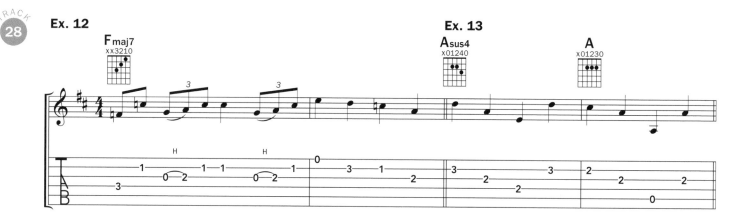

Taken by the Law

Words and music by Andrew DuBrock

Now let's try all of these together in a complete song! "Taken by the Law" uses this pattern as a guitar break *and* a verse backup, similar to the way Neil Young employs his passage in "Needle and the Damage Done." Continue working with these techniques, to come up with your own chordal riffs and guitar breaks. In the upcoming Single-Note Riffs and Backup lesson, we'll look at a different way to create rhythmic melodies and accompaniment by using single-note lines to craft riffs that drive songs.

* Guitar only, first time.

Alternating-Bass Fingerpicking

Many a talented thumb has held down the rhythm for countless rock, pop, and country songs using a technique called "alternating-bass fingerpicking." This method—in which you use your thumb to alternate between different bass notes—works great as a rolling rhythmic foundation for songs, and it has also been used by such guitarists as Chet Atkins and Jorma Kaukonen to create upbeat solo guitar pieces. The '60s wouldn't have been the same without Simon and Garfunkel, and many of their tunes provide great examples of alternating-bass fingerpicking. "The Boxer," "Homeward Bound," "Kathy's Song," and even the moody "For Emily Wherever I May Find Her" feature this technique. In this lesson, we'll learn how to get the essential alternating-bass patterns under our fingers, allowing us to create and play songs like Paul Simon did on some of his most enduring songs.

Combine Thumb and Fingers

Many fingerpickers start by assigning each picking-hand finger to one of the top three strings and repeating a rolling pattern while playing bass notes on the bottom three strings with the thumb, as in **Example 1**. The *p, m, i,* and *a* abbreviations represent Spanish-named fingerings: *pulgar* (thumb), *indice* (index), *medio* (middle), and *anular* (ring). In Example 1, your thumb stays on the low E string, as it does on the most basic fingerpicking patterns. Alternating-bass fingerpicking puts your thumb on double duty, requiring it to alternate between strings, as in **Example 2**. Spend some time with this example before moving on, and slow it down if you need to. It's important to get the thumb comfortable with alternating strings before you add anything else. Once you have this

The alternating thumb keeps the steady rhythm going while the fingers add notes on top.

groove under your fingers, it should thump along like a chugging train, keeping rock-steady rhythm. This rhythmic drive is part of what makes alternating-bass fingerpicking so effective for accompanying songs.

Now it's time to add your picking fingers. **Example 3** shows a common pattern, with your thumb playing every beat, and your index finger playing the third string on every offbeat. This may seem tricky at first, but it will help if you think about alternating notes between your thumb and index finger at a very slow tempo. Count "one-and two-and three-and four-and" as you play, and your index finger will be plucking notes every time you say "and." Break out the metronome if you're having trouble keeping a solid beat. Once you have Example 3 under your fingers, add your middle picking finger to the mix. **Example 4** shows a pattern similar to Example 3 that adds the middle finger on the second string.

The patterns we've just learned allow you to play a ton of songs, but let's add one more wrinkle. If you use your thumb to choose from three strings instead of two, you add another range of possibilities. **Example 5** shows one way to do this on an E chord by using your picking-hand thumb to alternate between the sixth and fourth strings in the first half of the measure and between the fifth and fourth strings during the second half of the measure. Notice how this changes the sound of the pattern: the previous patterns repeated themselves every two beats, whereas this modified alternating bass takes four beats. The new sequence of bass notes also adds a different color to the fingerpicking pattern because the B note on beat three is the fifth of the E chord—not the root of the chord, like every other bass note we've played up to

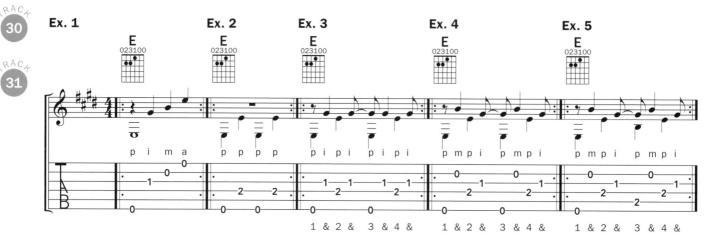

this point. The fifth of a chord doesn't support things quite as strongly, but it does help create motion—it sounds like things are rolling forward, rather than just rocking between root notes.

Add New Chords and Bass Notes

At this point, you can play a mean alternating-bass pattern on an E chord, but you need more than an E to play complete songs. While the alternating-bass pattern is similar for most chords, some chords will use different strings, depending on where their bass notes lie. For instance, on the E chord, your thumb alternated between the sixth and fourth strings, but for an A chord, try alternating between the *fifth* and fourth strings (**Example 6**). Note here that you're rocking between the root and fifth of the A in the bass, instead of alternating between roots, like you did on the E chord in Example 4. In Example 6 your thumb alternates between bass notes on two adjacent strings, so there isn't another string in between to create a three-string alternating-bass pattern like the one in Example 5. But if you include the open sixth string in your bass notes when playing the A chord, you can re-create the same three-string alternating-bass sound (**Example 7**). Here the root in the bass is followed by three fifths, which really accentuates the return of the root on the downbeat of each measure.

For a D chord, your fingers will pick the same pattern as they did with the A chord—you'll just have to move all your picking-hand fingers over one string, so your thumb plays the fourth and third strings (**Example 8**), alternating between the root and fifth in the bass. For a three-string alternating-bass pattern on D, simply move your picking-hand thumb down to the A string on beat three (**Example 9**). This pattern is similar to the A pattern in Example 7, since the bass plays the root followed by three fifths. An open-position C chord uses the same pattern as the A chord (**Example 10**), but notice that here you're alternating between the root and the third.

Playing a three-string alternating-bass pattern with a C chord is a bit tricky. You could move down to the low open-E string, but this sounds a little muddy with the C. Instead, start by fretting a C chord normally, and when beat three comes around (and it's time to play the bass note on the low E string), quickly move your fretting-hand ring finger from the third fret of the fifth string to the third fret of the low E string to play a G note (**Example 11**). This pattern may sound familiar to you as the backbone of the Simon and Garfunkel classic "The Boxer." You'll want to start moving your finger a little early—you can even start moving it during beat two, when your thumb is picking the fourth string. Once you've played the low note, move your ring finger back to the fifth string at the third fret during beat four so that it's ready to play the C note on the downbeat of the next measure. You could also play this pattern more easily by fretting it with four fingers: use your pinky to play the C note on the fifth string and grab the low G note with your ring finger. While this is technically a little easier, you'll find that people traditionally use the rocking ring finger method.

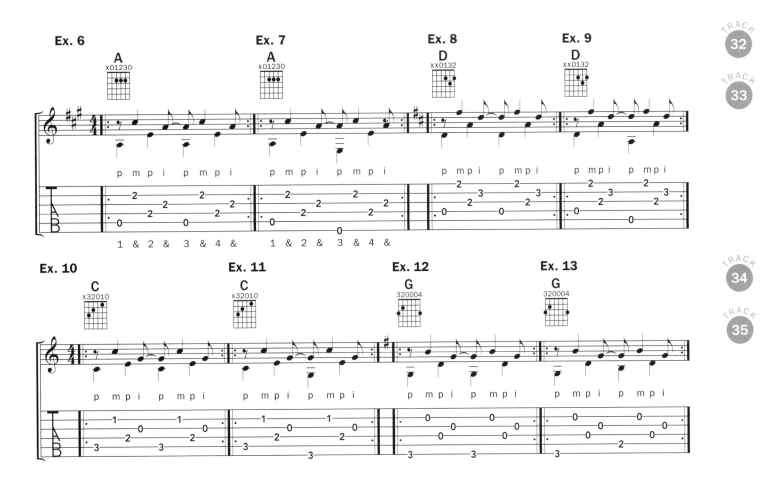

The G chord uses the same alternating-bass patterns as an E chord. **Example 12** shows a pattern using two strings for the bass, and **Example 13** shows a three-note alternating-bass pattern.

Picking with Pinches

Pinches add another texture to our alternating-bass patterns. To perform a pinch, play two notes simultaneously with your picking-hand thumb and a finger. In **Example 14**, there's a pinch on the first beat—a very common place for pinches. This pattern is similar to the fingerpicking pattern in Kansas's classic tune "Dust in the Wind," a part that started as an exercise guitarist Kerry Livgren came up with to help his students develop their alternating-bass fingerpicking skills.

Example 15 shows a different pinch placement—this time on beat two. You can pinch on any beat, and **Example 16** shows pinches on all four beats without any notes on the offbeats. **Example 17** adds offbeat notes to the pattern in Example 16; play these new notes with your index finger on the *ands* of beats two and four.

Now let's look at a complete song that uses all our newfound alternating-bass picking techniques. "The Troubadour"

In this pinch, the thumb picks the sixth string and the middle finger simultaneously picks the second string.

uses fingerpicking patterns and chords similar to those Paul Simon used in "The Boxer." The song starts on a C chord with the challenging three-note alternating-bass pattern, so this is a great song for practicing that pattern. The song uses patterns and chords we've already covered until you hit the Csus2/B chord in measure 10. Don't worry about the complicated-sounding name. This is really just a passing chord that moves from the Am to the C, a common tool used to join these chords. Just leave your index finger on the second string at the first fret, lift your middle and ring fingers, and place your middle finger on the second fret of the fifth string while you continue the picking pattern. There are no more surprises until the chorus, where you play pinches on the second beats of measures 21, 23, and 25. For the most part, the rolling feel of straight alternating-bass fingerpicking fits this song well, but the brief break we get with these pinches provides a nice contrast to the motion of the rest of the tune.

Try applying these patterns to songs you already know or creating your own tunes. And experiment with your own patterns by putting pinches in different places or using your index and middle fingers at different times throughout a measure.

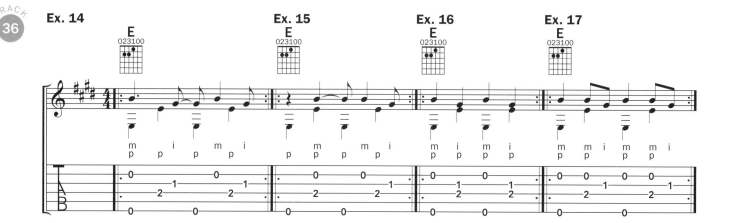

The Troubadour

Words and music by Andrew DuBrock

Intro

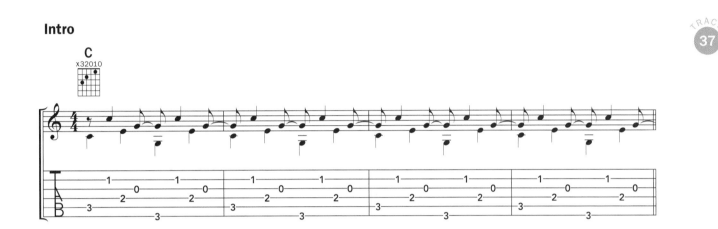

Verse

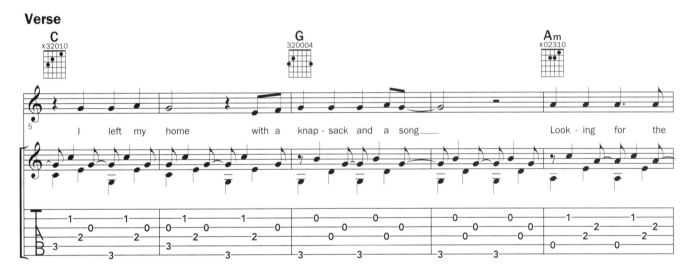

I left my home with a knap-sack and a song____ Look-ing for the

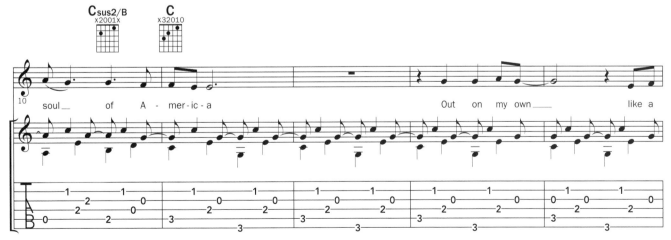

soul __ of A - mer-ic-a   Out on my own ____ like a

Single-Note Riffs and Backup

Dave Matthews's "Satellite" opens with an ear-catching single-note line; it's the riff and the vocal backup—the thread that weaves the song together. Single-note riffs like this are distinct and catchy, and they're different from chordal riffs (which I covered in the Creating Chordal Riffs lesson), because they use single notes exclusively to provide the melody and often the accompaniment for a song. When you hear a passage like this, the sheer number of notes can be intimidating; how do you create such cool but complicated lines out of thin air? Most great single-note riffs have a simple idea behind them, though, and when you break them down—or start from a small piece and build them up—they become much more manageable. In this lesson, we're going to look at three ways you can create riffs out of bite-size pieces and build single-note riffs like those used by Matthews and the Police's Andy Summers in some of their best songs.

Static Riff, Moving Melody

The first approach we'll try takes a small idea—a "riff fragment"—and adapts it to work across a chord progression, turning it into a full-blown accompaniment for a tune. You don't need to start with much. For instance, come up with one small idea you like—something short, like **Example 1**. We'll be working

in the key of D, so let's experiment with expanding the riff to fit over a measure of D—a little repetition, as shown in **Example 2**, will work. This doesn't sound like much yet, but we've essentially built our riff. Now all we have to do is apply it to a full song or chord progression.

Let's work with a G–D–A–D chord progression in the key of D. To make the idea work over those other chords, make small adjustments to the strong notes of the riff—the longer F♯ notes [on beats one, three, and four]—that will conflict with the G and A chords. Over a G chord, we'll move that F♯ note up to a G note (**Example 3**), and for the A chord, we'll slide that F♯ down to an E (**Example 4**); notice how each of these riff fragments matches the chords a little better because we've changed the discordant notes to chord tones that fit each background chord. Once you string these ideas together to fit the chord progression, and you've got a full-blown riff! **Example 5** shows the fruits of our labor. If it sounds familiar to you, that's because it's very similar to Dave Matthews's riff in "Ants Marching." Not all riffs require a rhythm guitar, but this particular one will sound much fuller with a backing rhythm, so recruit a friend to play rhythm and you can hear it in all its glory!

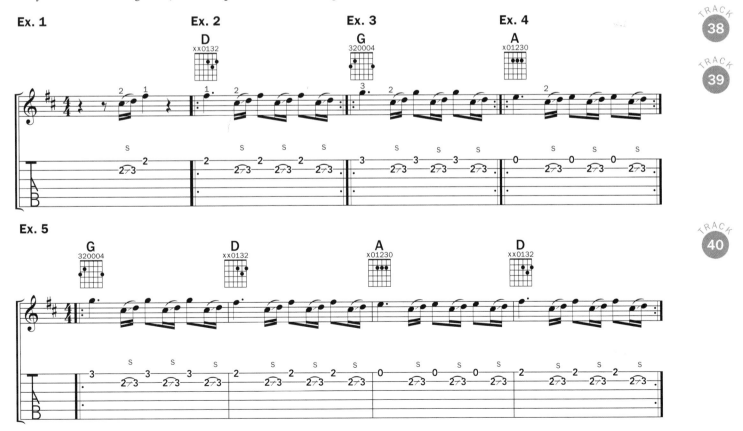

Move Riff Fragments to Follow Chords

We've just looked at creating riffs by adapting a fragment to each chord in a progression. You can also move the *whole* riff fragment into place for each chord in a progression. Let's start with the E-minor fragment in **Example 6**—an interesting open-sounding segment that's a bit of a finger stretcher, but worth the extra work. Try playing the first note with your index finger, the second note with your middle finger, and reach up with your pinky for the high note at the eleventh fret. Next, we'll match that riff to an Em–D–C–Am chord progression; all we have to do is slide the phrase down (or up) the fretboard to follow each chord. Note that our fragment started on an E note over the Em chord; we're going to play the same fragment over every other chord—it's just moved so that the first note of each riff matches the chord name: the D fragment starts on D, the C fragment starts on C, and the Am fragment starts on A. So for the D chord, move your index finger down two frets to the seventh fret (**Example 7**), for the C chord, slide down two more frets to start on the C note on the third fret (**Example 8**), and for the final Am chord, move down to the fifth fret of the sixth string (**Example 9**).

It's worth noting that not all riff fragments you come up with will be this easy to move—this one is because the root, fifth, and ninth of the corresponding chord sounds good when moved around in this context. Other scale degrees may conflict with the underlying chord when moving the riff around, so always use your ear. For instance, if you're using a major third in your fragment and it sounds bad when you move it, try using a minor third instead (or even substitute another interval that's close to that third every time it sounds strange). It all comes down to what sounds good to you.

To complete the riff, move those fragments into the chord progression (**Example 10**) and add some minor rhythmic variations. You'll note that the chord changes happen to perfectly match each riff's eighth-note rhythm, which creates a neat syncopated feel ("syncopation" is when weak beats are accented—like the *and* of beats two and four in the first measure of Example 10, which are accented by chord changes). Also note how the Am fragment runs out an eighth note before the end of the measure. I've added a slide up to the 10th fret for two reasons: it helps you get back in position to repeat the riff and it sounds cool! If this riff sounds vaguely familiar, that's because it's similar to what Andy Summers used on the Police's huge hit "Message in a Bottle."

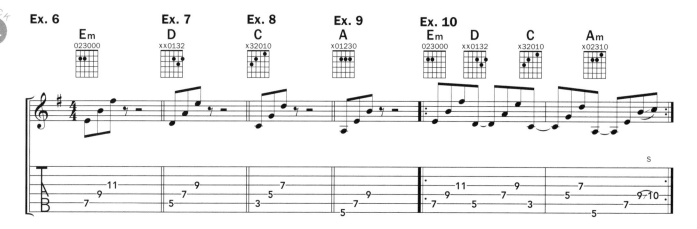

Forget the Chords!

Our final riff-constructing method moves fragments around to different sets of strings or other places on the neck in the same way we previously did. However, this method doesn't involve creating a riff specifically to fit an underlying chord structure, like our method for examples 6–9. Instead, we'll just create a fragment that sounds interesting, not worrying about the chord progression. Often, this approach ends up creating meditative riffs that suggest a single background chord, and they usually don't need any type of chordal accompaniment.

We'll approach this exercise the way Dave Matthews might have approached creating the riff to his song "Satellite." We'll start again with a small fragment—**Example 11**—similar to what we used in our previous examples (and a riff we know is easily movable because we've done it above!). The key to this technique is to start with your fragment and take part—or all—of it and move it around. We'll start by simply transposing the pattern from Example 11 over to the next set of strings, as shown in **Example 12**. Next, I've taken a part of it—the last three notes—and continued sliding those over, to the fourth and third strings (**Example 13**) so that when I add them to the two other fragments, they fill out the measure (**Example 14**). It's a simple concept, but the resulting riff is nice, and has a lot of similarities to Dave Matthews's "Satellite." Once you have a moving part like this down, you can transpose it all to one position, as in (**Example 15**). This is how Matthews plays his "Satellite" riff, and—while it may be easier in the long run for backing up a vocal because you won't have to move your fretting hand quite as much—I actually find it a bit harder than Example 13. The key is to use what works best for you in any context, so if you can make a riff easier, then by all means *do it!* You could even try moving the riff down to open position (**Example 16**), which has different challenges.

We don't need much more to spin this riff into a complete song. "Sunlight" on page 42 uses the pattern for an intro and virtually all of the verse. At the end of the intro, notice the short pause to accentuate the vocal's entrance. You'll see this same technique used between vocal phrases (measure 8), and you can hear Dave Matthews employing a similar pause in "Satellite." A few strummed chords in measures 11–13 are all we need to contrast the riff. Notice how much fresher the return of the riff in measure 14 sounds after this break.

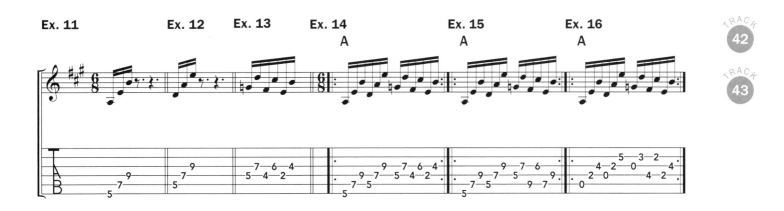

TRACK 42

TRACK 43

Sunlight

Words and music by Andrew DuBrock

Intro

Verse

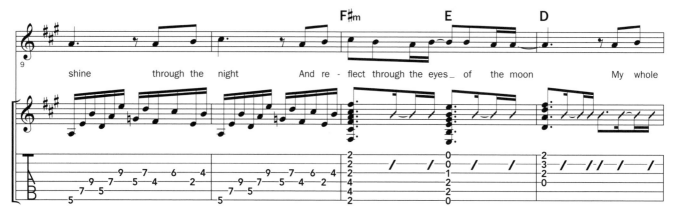

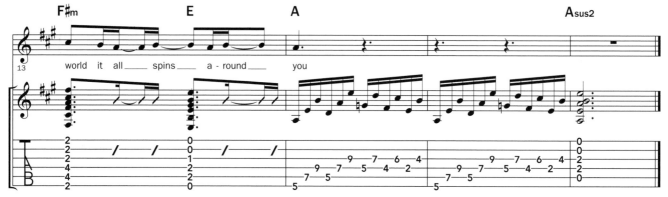

Percussive Rhythm Techniques

Adding percussion to a song can enhance its rhythm, turning a flat arrangement into a three-dimensional soundscape. Of course, hiring a drummer or percussionist isn't a luxury we all have—especially solo guitar players and singer-songwriters. But your guitar has percussive qualities of its own. Pop and rock masters like Jack Johnson, Dave Matthews, and the classic '70s band Boston have used percussive guitar techniques on some of their chart-topping songs, and you can learn how to easily integrate these ideas into your playing, too.

In this lesson, we'll explore how to play percussive strums called scratch rhythms to keep a song's pulse bouncing forward. Then we'll touch on a few more advanced techniques—like picking-hand tapping and body slapping—to see how to add more drum-like effects to your songs.

Scratch Rhythm

Scratch rhythms involve strumming across muted strings, producing a scratchy percussive sound that can add energy to any strum pattern or inject character into a riff. To play scratch rhythm, damp the strings by lightly laying your fretting-hand fingers across the strings as shown in the photo, then strum, as shown in

Flatten your fretting-hand fingers to damp the strings when playing scratch rhythm.

Example 1. (The X's in the tab and notation indicate muted notes.) This creates a scratch rhythm across all six strings. Make sure you're pressing down hard enough to completely damp the strings, but not so hard that you hear any notes sounding—when you strum, you should hear a percussive "chucka chucka" sound. If you hear any open strings ringing, press down a little more to damp the strings. If you hear fretted notes, loosen up a little on the damping, and if you hear bell-like harmonics, slide your fretting hand up or down the strings until the harmonics go away.

Now let's combine scratch rhythm with some chord strums. **Example 2** alternates four eighth-note strums of a D chord with four eighth-note scratch-rhythm strums. Strum the D chord for two beats, lift your fingers off the chord to damp the strings for two beats, and press down again to hear the D chord when you repeat the process in measure 2. Once you're comfortable playing through Example 2, practice alternating between the D chord for two eighth notes and scratch rhythms for two eighth notes. Then try alternating every eighth note.

Working scratch-rhythm strums into chord progressions keeps the rhythm driving forward. **Example 3** shows one way

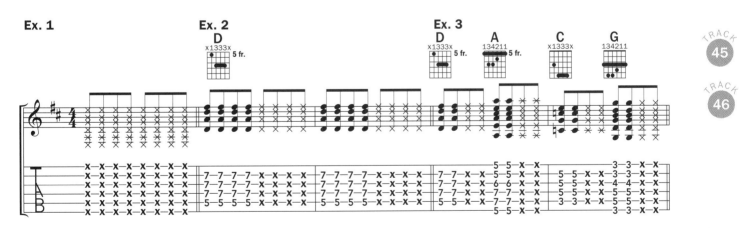

you could apply this technique to a D–A–C–G progression, similar to the guitar break on Boston's classic "Long Time."

Now let's use scratch rhythm to emulate a real percussion instrument—the snare drum. In most 4/4 pop songs, the drummer hits the snare on beats two and four, which adds extra snap. **Example 4** shows how to approximate this sound when you're playing by yourself—just throw in scratch-rhythm strums on beats two and four. Note that you need to mute the open strings when playing scratch rhythm on a C chord. To do this, slap the heel of your picking hand against the strings on beats two and four at the same time your pick hits the strings. This produces a much more pronounced "chuck" sound than standard scratch rhythm, and the extra force helps create a sound like the rattling snap of a snare. Many pop/rock artists use this technique to drive their songs. Example 4 would work well when playing a solo version of Creedence Clearwater Revival's "Have You Ever Seen the Rain?"

and other mid-tempo or upbeat 4/4 tunes. **Example 5** shows a chord progression similar to Jack Johnson's hit "Sitting, Waiting, Wishing" with scratch rhythm on beats two and four.

So far, we've used the scratch-rhythm technique on chords, but you can also use it to play single-note lines—just pick one string while you damp it. **Example 6** shows how you can create funky licks by using the scratch-rhythm technique on a single-note line. The rhythm is a bit tricky, so take this slowly at first, and if you have problems, count along using 16th-note subdivisions.

Tapping and Slapping

Another way to add percussive drive to your guitar parts is to tap or slap the strings or top of the guitar. When rock guitarists hear the word "tapping," they often think of the lead technique where the picking hand taps notes on the fretboard, as in **Example 7**. Pick the first note with your picking hand, but use hammer-ons

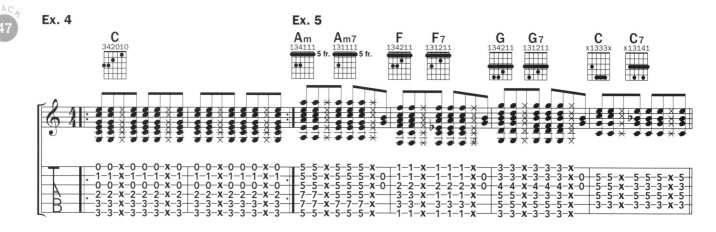

TRACK 48

TRACK 49

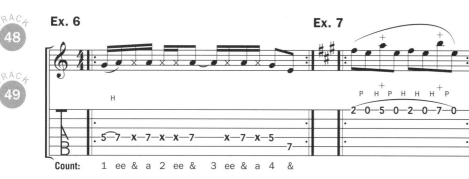

Use your picking-hand index or middle finger for tapping.

and pull-offs to play the rest of the example. The "tapping" occurs on the notes with a "+" over them. Move your picking hand to the indicated fret, hammer-on with a picking-hand finger, and pull-off to sound the open string. Use the middle finger of your picking hand to tap if you're holding a pick, or use either the index or middle finger of your picking hand if you're playing fingerstyle.

While this is a nice way to add fluidity to single-note lines, let's explore some other percussive tapping techniques. **Example 8** shows percussive double-stop picking-hand slaps on beat two of each measure. Strum the Em chord and reach over the top of the fretboard with your picking hand to slap the double-stops on the fifth and seventh frets with the fleshy pad or side of your index or middle finger. Hit the fifth and sixth strings firmly just behind the fret wire to sound the notes clearly. This technique provides some percussive pop while you hold the Em chord with your fretting-hand fingers.

Slap Harmonics

The percussive technique known as "slap harmonics" creates a percussive sound combined with bell-like tones. Use your picking hand to slap any string where it usually produces harmonics—most commonly on the fifth, seventh, and 12th frets. You can also slap 12 frets above any fretted notes (and even five or seven frets above fretted notes). **Example 9** shows this technique on the 12th fret, using the same Em–D–Em chord progression in Example 8. Strum and hold the Em chord, and slap the 12th fret across the top three strings, making sure your hand hits directly over the fret wire, instead of behind it. Use the flat, fleshy pad of your picking-hand index or middle finger, and listen for the bell-like harmonic tone. If you hear thuds or toneless slapping, you're not hitting right on the fret wire. Don't worry about how many strings you hit. This technique isn't as much about precision as it is about the ear-popping harmonic. Follow this slap with another slap on

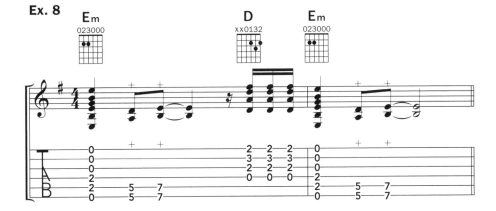

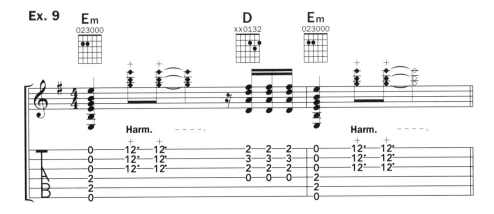

the 12th fret before strumming the D chord and repeating the slaps. Once you can play these slap harmonics at the 12th fret, try them at the fifth and seventh frets, too.

The Guitar as a Drum

Your guitar's body and soundboard amplify the sound of the strings, but it can also act as a percussive box—a drum. Try slapping or tapping the soundboard or side of your guitar with either hand to add a drum-like sound to your rhythm guitar parts. **Example 10** shows one way to do this. In this example, the hollow squares represent a slap on the guitar's side, along the lower bout. Perform this slap with the fingers of your fretting hand. The hollow triangles represent a slap on the soundboard (again on the lower bout). If you're playing fingerstyle, use your thumb for

this slap (which should be in perfect position after the finger slap on the side). If you're holding a pick, try using the the heel of your hand for this slap. There are nearly limitless ways to slap and tap the soundboard and sides of your guitar, so experiment and find the ways you like best.

Now let's try a song that uses percussive techniques. "Right About You" uses scratch rhythms on the offbeats to create a percussive backdrop similar to some of Jack Johnson's biggest hits. This technique is used throughout the song to give it a constantly driving feel. The trickiest moves are the slapped harmonics in measures 19–20. I strum this song with a pick, so I can't use the index finger of my picking hand to slap the harmonics. I slap the strings with my middle finger instead.

TRACK 51

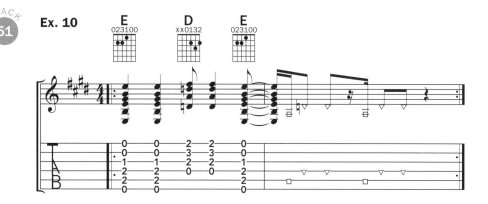

Slap the side of your guitar for a drum-like effect.

Slap the lower bout with your thumb when playing fingerstyle.

You can also slap the lower bout with the heel of your hand.

Right About You

Words and music by Andrew DuBrock

48 ACOUSTIC ROCK GUITAR BASICS

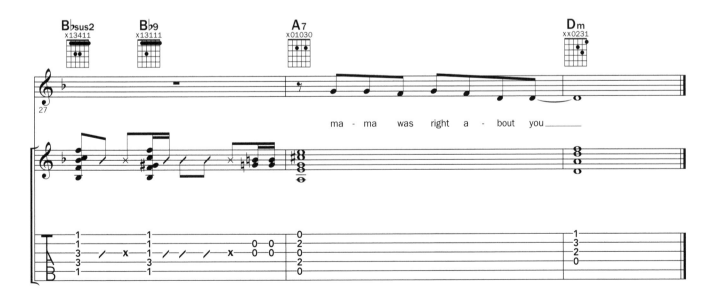

Alternate Tunings in Acoustic Rock

Standard tuning can be a huge security blanket. Tweak a tuning knob, and many guitarists will run for the hills. But exploring alternate tunings automatically inspires you to play the guitar in a different way and can introduce you to sounds you might not discover in standard tuning. Some of the most prominent pop and rock guitarists of our time created some of their greatest guitar work in alternate tunings. Songs like Led Zeppelin's "Black Mountain Side" and "Bron-Y-Aur," Fleetwood Mac's "Never Going Back Again," and Crosby, Stills, Nash, and Young's "Suite: Judy Blue Eyes" are just a few iconic examples. In this lesson, we'll take a look at a few types of alternate tunings and explore how guitar tunings and techniques were adapted from older folk and blues traditions to the pop and rock world.

Dropped-D Tuning

Dropped-D tuning, in which the low E string is tuned down ("dropped") a whole step to D, is a great place to start your alternate-tuning journey. This small change makes D chords sound huge, because you can play the low, open D string, along with the open A string, for a six-string D chord (at right).

And because this tuning affects only the sixth string, any chord that doesn't use that string can be played exactly the same as in standard tuning—C, A, Am, B7, etc. Any chord that uses the sixth string will need some adjustment because that string is now tuned down a whole step. So you'll need to fret the sixth string up two frets (a whole step) from where you'd fret it in standard tuning. For example, see E and G at right.

D
000132

E
234100
G
3x0001

Dropped-D tuning has been popular among folk and Celtic players—some of whom have been influential in rock circles. One example is Scottish folk guitarist Bert Jansch, whose arrangement of the traditional Irish tune "Blackwaterside" uses a fingerstyle lick similar to **Example 1**. Jimmy Page adapted Jansch's arrangement to D A D G A D tuning, calling his solo guitar version "Black Mountain Side"—a popular acoustic track for Led Zeppelin.

Techniques from other instruments are also sometimes easier to transfer to guitar in alternate tunings. The banjo, for instance, is played in tunings similar to some alternate tunings on guitar. Lindsey Buckingham took banjo roll patterns and turned them into alternating-bass fingerpicking patterns on guitar for songs like "Never Going Back Again," which he plays in dropped-D tuning. **Example 2** is similar to what Buckingham played on that Fleetwood Mac track. The alternating-bass fingerpicking that includes the low D on the sixth string is easy to *see* in the down-stemmed bass notes in the notation, but the rolls in measures 5–7 are harder to spot. Look at the up-stemmed portion of the notation in Example 2. This is just a slowed-down version of a sequence like **Example 3**, where the roll pattern is much easier to see and play. And if you want to sound even more like Buckingham, try the reverse roll pattern in **Example 4**. In "Never Going Back Again" Buckingham also uses a common move in standard tuning—alternating a barred A chord and a D/A chord (**Example 5**)—that works even better in dropped D. If you reverse the order of the chords, the low D bass note makes this progression sound huge (**Example 6**).

Ex. 1

Ex. 3   **Ex. 4**

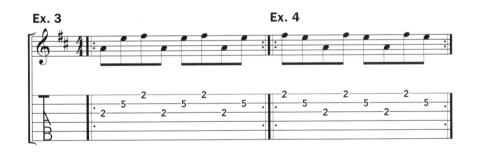

Ex. 5   **Ex. 6**

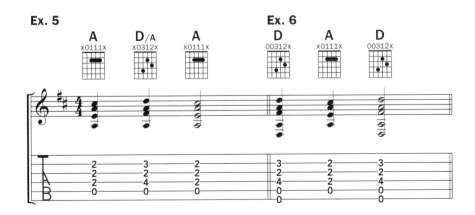

Common Alternate Tunings

While there are countless alternate tunings, the ones you'll see most often are:

- Dropped D (D A D G B E)
- Double dropped-D (D A D G B D)
- D A D G A D

Other alternate tunings you may run across are:

- G6 (D G D G B E)
- C G C G C D

The most common open tunings are:

- Open G (D G D G B D)
- Open D (D A D F♯ A D)

Other popular open tunings include:

- Open E (E B E G♯ B E)
- Open A (E A E A C♯ E)
- Open C (C G C G C E)
- Open G minor (D G D G B♭ D)
- Open D minor (D A D F A D).

TRACK 54

TRACK 55

TRACK 56

TRACK 57

D A D G A D

Dropped D feels like familiar territory because you've only changed one of the strings. The more you turn those tuning gears the more it feels like you're transforming your guitar into a new instrument. D A D G A D tuning deviates from standard tuning more than dropped D by dropping the B and high E strings a whole step, to A and D, respectively. With three strings retuned, chord shapes don't resemble those in standard tuning anymore:

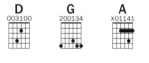

But this is where we start seeing the magic of alternate tunings. Modified versions of these chords with ringing open strings are often much easier to play than their standard-tuning major or minor versions. One reason for this is that the notes of D A D G A D spell out a suspended chord—meaning that it's not major or minor. So the ringing open strings in D A D G A D work well in major or minor keys and have an ambiguously open sound if you decide to avoid specific major or minor chords. In fact, the tuning seems to urge you to play anything but standard major or minor shapes. For example, try these three chords instead of the D, G, and A chords above:

D A D G A D is popular in Celtic and modern fingerstyle guitar circles, where open, suspended sounds and an ambiguity between major and minor keys is common. It was also a favorite tuning of British folk guitarist Davey Graham. Jimmy Page was heavily influenced by Graham, borrowing some of his arrangements to create the Led Zeppelin song "White Summer" and following Graham's lead by using D A D G A D on songs like "Black Mountain Side," a version of Jansch's "Blackwaterside" (which we looked at in dropped-D tuning in Example 1). **Example 7** is

similar to Page's D A D G A D version. Notice how Page moved the pull-off in the second beat over one string (from the fourth string in the Jansch-style Example 1 to the third string here), resulting in higher notes and putting Page's unique stamp on the song.

There are countless other alternate tunings to explore (see "Common Alternate Tunings" on page 51 for a few of the most common), but D A D G A D is one of the most popular, and you'll come across it more than nearly any other. Some guitarists—like modern fingerstyle master Pierre Bensusan—use D A D G A D exclusively as their "standard tuning."

Open Tunings

Within the vast group of existing alternate tunings lies a subset called *open tunings*, in which the strings are tuned to a major or minor chord. As you may guess, these are great for playing huge open chords, but finding other chords is easy, too—simply barre across all six strings at frets up and down the neck and you instantly get other chords (see "Instant Chords in Open Tunings" on page 53). This makes open tunings great for slide playing.

Open-G tuning (D G D G B D) is one of the more popular open tunings, especially in blues circles. Rolling Stones guitarist Keith Richards was heavily influenced by country blues guitarists and used open-G tuning for many of the Rolling Stones' biggest hits. In open-G tuning, the two chord shapes at right work well together.

Richards uses these chords so often that you can re-create most of his signature licks by playing the shapes together and sliding them around the fretboard. Try **Example 8** to get a feel for it, then go knock off as many Richards-style riffs as you can on your own!

Ex. 7
Tuning: D A D G A D

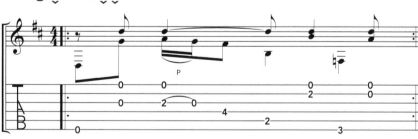

Ex. 8
Open G Tuning: D G D G B D

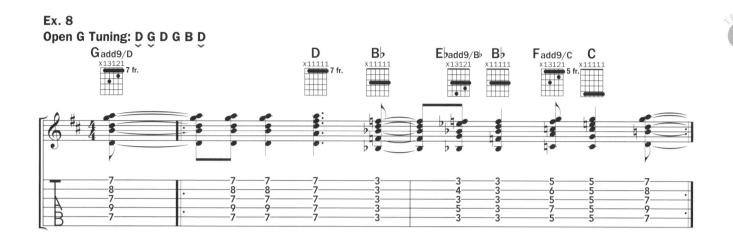

TRACK
59

Unusual Tunings

Once you start turning the tuning knobs, it can be hard to stop. Some artists take more common open and alternate tunings and make small adjustments to them for a slightly different sound. Others create a tuning from scratch that works perfectly for a certain song. You can end up with some very strange tunings—things like E E E E B E, which Stephen Stills used on Crosby, Stills, Nash, and Young's "Suite: Judy Blue Eyes," or D A D A A E, which Johnny Rzeznik used on the Goo Goo Dolls' "Name."

In odd tunings like this, experimentation can be a great way to get going. Try using chord shapes from other tunings or small shapes and chords with only one fretted note. But make sure to use a lot of open strings—that's where the magic of alternate tunings lies.

When Jimmy Page wrote the Led Zeppelin song "Bron-Y-Aur," he used a tuning similar to open-C tuning (C G C G C E), but with

the fifth string tuned to A (C A C G C E). Let's try a full song that uses this tuning: "Llanfair."

In the opening measures, notice how the tuning allows for a nice slide up to the third fret on the fifth string to play the unison C note against the open C on the fourth string. This is similar to the move Page uses in "Bron-Y-Aur," and it's possible this is why he tuned the fifth string to A. Most of "Llanfair" is built on four-measure phrases that are pieced together. Notice how some sections—like the passage in measures 13–16—slide similar chord shapes around to build a phrase, modifying individual chords to suit the sound at the moment. The section in measures 13–16 repeats at measure 33. At this point, my ear wanted to extend this line, so I ended up with the long passage in measures 39–49. Notice that the shapes are similar but have been modified in the extended line to serve the melody and harmony.

TRACK
60

Instant Chords in Open Tunings

Open tunings may seem intimidating at first, since the notes of your guitar are tuned quite differently than in standard tuning. But since the strings are tuned to the notes of a chord, playing slide or barre chords all over the neck is much easier than in standard tuning—simply lay your slide or barre your index finger across all six strings. The most common chords used in songs are the I, IV, and V chords and—no matter what open tuning you're in—these chords will always fall in the same place on your guitar: play the open strings or barre at the 12th fret for the I chord, barre at the fifth fret for the IV chord, and barre at the seventh fret for the V chord.

Llanfair

Words and music by Andrew DuBrock

Expand Your Fingerpicking Accompaniment

Fingerpicking patterns are a great way to back up your songs, in part because they allow you and the listener to focus on the vocal line. They're also relatively easy to play while you're singing because your pinking-hand fingers can repeat the same movements throughout a verse, chorus, or even an entire song. (See the Alternating-Bass Fingerpicking lesson for an introduction to pattern picking.) But there are times when you may want more variation in your guitar parts—between verses, during instrumental breaks, or even *during* the vocals to accent a vocal phrase—and breaking out of standard fingerpicking patterns is a great way to accomplish this. When you move beyond pattern playing, a whole new world of fingerpicking opens up, and it gives you the flexibility to vary the sound and dynamics of your playing in the blink of an eye. That flexibility is what gives songs like James Taylor's "Fire and Rain" or Cat Stevens's "Moonshadow" their distinctive sound.

In this lesson, you'll learn a few new ways to expand your fingerpicking repertoire by adding fills, bass runs, pauses, and other effects to some common fingerpicking patterns. And you'll learn a song that uses fingerpicking ideas similar to those Taylor used in songs like "Country Road."

Mix Your Patterns

The challenge of playing without patterns is as much mental as physical, because you have to spend more time *thinking* about how you're playing at any given moment. But part of it is physically training your fingers to break free of patterns they're very used to playing. A great way to start is by simply mixing patterns. For instance, **Example 1** uses an alternating-bass fingerpicking pattern for the first half of the measure, and then switches to a roll pattern in the second half. Use your picking-hand thumb on the fifth and fourth strings and your index, middle, and ring fingers on the third, second, and first strings, respectively. Repeat this example until your thumb and fingers are comfortable switching between patterns fluidly and in time. Next, try the similar pattern in **Example 2**. In this pattern, assign your thumb and fingers to the same strings as in Example 1. For the roll starting midway through the measure, note that instead of your index finger playing the second note of the roll pattern, your thumb does double duty, moving between the fifth and fourth strings twice as fast as in the previous example.

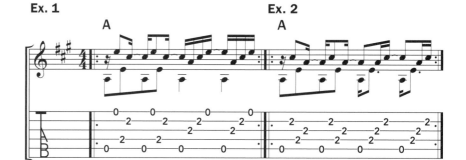

Manipulate the Bass and Add Fills

Another way you can create variations in your fingerpicking is by giving your thumb a rest every so often, which removes bass notes from the pattern. Start with the alternating-bass picking pattern in **Example 3**, and eliminate thumb notes on the second, third, and fourth beats of the measure, as shown in **Example 4**. Notice how this makes the accompaniment sound as if it's pausing—a great way to make a measure or two stand out before returning to the alternating-bass pattern.

Now let's go back to the full picking pattern in Example 3 and add a fill similar to one James Taylor often uses (**Example 5**). Notice how the bass drops out here on beat four so that the melody line of the fill sticks out more. To thicken the fill and sound even more like Taylor, we can add double-stops (**Example 6**).

In the previous examples, bass notes were omitted to create a brief pause in the underlying pulse, but there are also times you may want to add extra bass notes. The pattern in **Example 7** uses half notes in the bass against an eighth-note pattern in the fingers, and a chordal fill (again reminiscent of Taylor) in the second mea-

sure. But something sounds a little off in that last measure—the syncopated melody notes feel strange against such a sparse backdrop, so in **Example 8** I added bass notes to fill out the rhythm. In this example, *adding* bass notes accentuates the fill, while in other instances, omitting bass notes can highlight a fill.

Support the Song

Once you're comfortable switching between patterns, omitting or adding bass notes, and introducing melodies and fills, you've successfully broken away from strict pattern playing. From here on, the goal is to support the song you're playing the best you can. Sometimes that may mean a lot of pattern picking, and sometimes it may mean playing very few patterns. Behind vocal melodies, for example, patterns often work well because they allow you to focus more on your singing. Their repetitive nature also ensures they won't take away from the vocals by distracting the listener. But short fills between vocal lines, like the one in **Example 9**, can be a nice contrast.

Ex. 3   **Ex. 4**

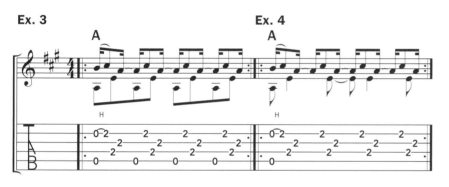

TRACK 63

Ex. 5   **Ex. 6**

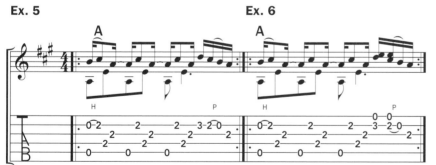

TRACK 64

Ex. 7   **Ex. 8**

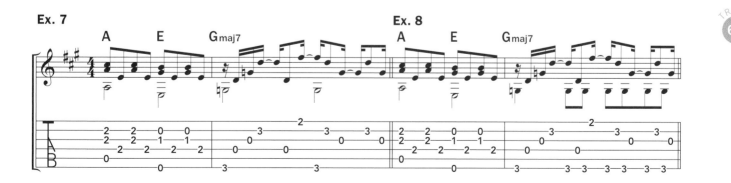

TRACK 65

During intros, interludes, and instrumental sections, you may have a melody in mind that you want to play along with the accompaniment. The key is to know the melody you want and construct the accompaniment appropriately. You'll naturally fall out of prescribed fingerpicking patterns as you go. For instance, let's take the rhythmic melody line in **Example 10**, which uses rhythms similar to James Taylor's "Country Road," and add a fill on the end. We could add bass notes on the beat, as in **Example 11**, but this sounds a bit stiff, so let's try following the chords more closely, playing a bass note with each chord, as in **Example 12**. It's still a bit underwhelming—I often find that bass lines sound best when they're rhythmically independent from the melody, but accent the melody by coming together at key points, as in **Example 13**. Here, every note in the bass is played independently of the melody except during the resolve to the A chord on the "and" of beat two, just before the fill.

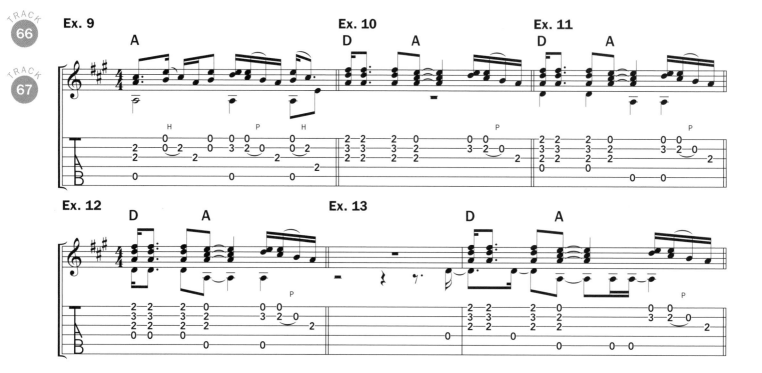

Break of Day

Words and music by Andrew DuBrock

Now that you're comfortable varying what your picking-hand thumb and fingers are doing, let's explore even more possibilities in a full song. "Break of Day" uses all the techniques we've tried and is similar to several James Taylor songs. Notice how the accompaniment tends to stick closer to pattern playing behind the vocals, breaking away for fills between vocal lines (measures 8–9, 14, 16, and 18). The intro breaks out of patterns the most and is also the trickiest part to play. It starts with a sliding D-shape chord on the top three strings. Watch for all the hammer-

ons and pull-offs in measure 2—particularly the one on beat three, because it's hard to keep the second string ringing while you play a pull-off. Don't worry too much if you mute that note. You can pluck the string again with your ring finger as it pulls off of the third string—essentially plucking the string in the motion of pulling off. Check out how measure 4 uses the same chords and rhythms as Example 13, except here we use a pedal A bass note for a different sound.

Played with a full band, then played without the band.

TRACK 68

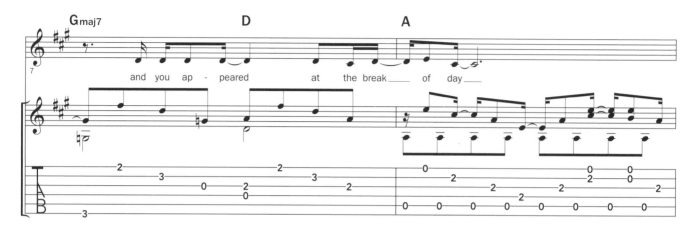

and you ap - peared   at   the break ____ of   day ____

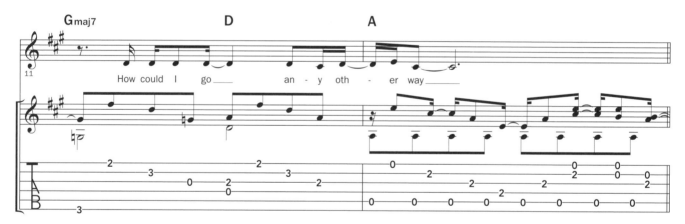

You were head-in' down the val - ley   or where - ev - er the wind   blows ____

How could I   go ____   an - y oth - er way ____

Chorus

Now I   take   the good days   with ___ the bad ____   There are

man - y you could say were the best I ev - er had _____ I've known

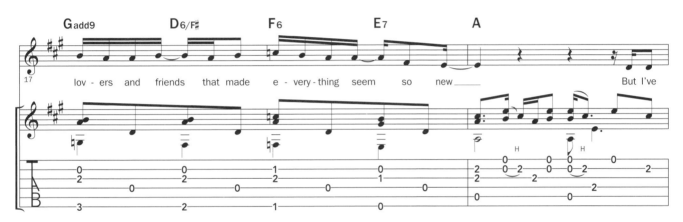

lov - ers and friends that made e - very - thing seem so new _____ But I've

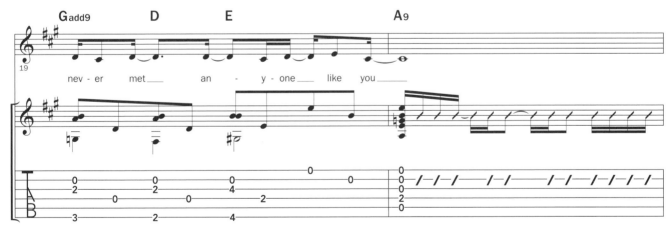

nev - er met _____ an - y - one _____ like you _____

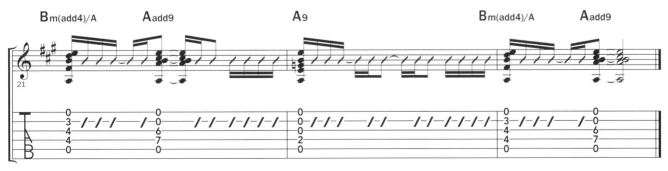

Soloing with Pentatonic Scales

With so many notes on your guitar's fretboard, it can be hard to know which ones to use to craft a solo. But here's a little secret: artists like Eric Clapton, Jimmy Page, and Duane Allman often used only five notes to create some of the greatest solos of all time, employing the magic of the *minor-pentatonic* scale and its close relative, the *major-pentatonic* scale.

Pentatonic means "five notes," and that's part of the reason these scales are a great place to start. Many other scales use seven notes, so you have fewer notes to keep track of with pentatonics. But the main reason people use pentatonic scales is to create dynamic solos. In this lesson, we'll learn a movable shape for both major and minor pentatonic scales that you can transpose to any key—enabling you to play solos on a huge number of songs. We'll start with the most popular of the two: the minor-pentatonic scale.

The Minor-Pentatonic Scale

You hear songs that use the minor-pentatonic scale in nearly every genre of music, and, because it lends a bluesy sound to solos, it's especially popular with blues players. **Example 1** shows the five notes that make up the A-minor-pentatonic scale. The starting note of any scale is the *root*. The minor-pentatonic scale also includes the flat-third, fourth, fifth, and flat-seventh degrees. Those flatted notes (the flat-third and flat-seventh) add a darker

tone than their nonflatted counterparts do. They're part of what gives the blues its sound.

Notice that the sixth note in this example is also the root. Once you reach the end of any scale, it cycles back to the root, and you can continue up the scale as far as you like (or as far as you can go on your instrument). Playing in fifth position, you can cycle through a little more than two full minor-pentatonic scales in the key of A (**Example 2**). Once you learn Example 2, you can play a minor-pentatonic scale in any key! That's because this is the movable minor-pentatonic shape we talked about at the beginning of this lesson (see "Building Pentatonic Scales in Any Key" on page 66 to learn how to do this).

Example 3 shows a lick over an A-major chord progression that will help get you started. One of the beauties of this scale is that it works in both a minor *and* a major context. As you'd expect, it works in a minor key because it *is* minor. But it also works in a major key because the discordant flat-third and flat-seventh notes create hip harmonies against the background chords. For the three most common chords in a key, the most discordant moments will create the flat-fifth (a bluesy sound) and a flat-ninth (the note that gives Jimi Hendrix's "Purple Haze" its distinctive sound). **Example 4** shows the same lick played over a minor chord progression. Once you have the notes under your fingers, try using the scale to come up with your own licks.

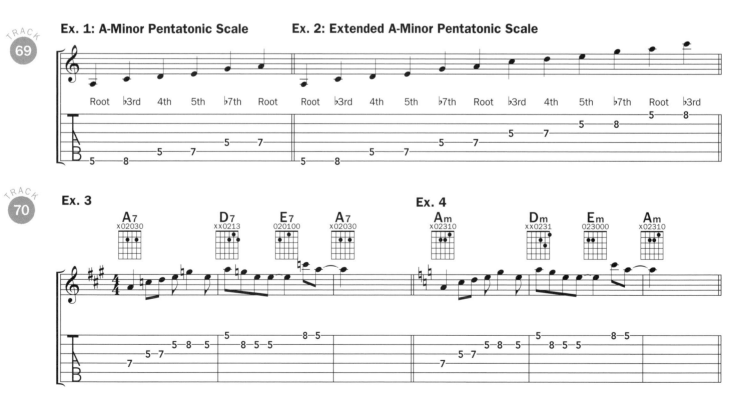

And what if someone plays the chord progression in G instead of A? No problem!—this pattern works anywhere on the fretboard. Just move down two frets, and you can play the same lick in the key of G (**Example 5**).

Building a Minor-Pentatonic Solo

Let's finish our introduction to the minor-pentatonic scale by walking through a complete blues solo: "Solo Blue." In the process, you'll learn a few tricks to help you come up with interesting lead lines. The solo starts with a few eighth-note lines, but notice that it's not just continuous, uninterrupted eighth notes. Lead lines sound best when they "breathe" a little: think about a singer pausing for breath, and it will hold you back from playing a constant flurry of notes. To see what I mean, look at measure 3, where I've held one note through the measure. Combined with

the whole-note rest in measure 4, that's a two-measure pause! You don't always have to pause this much, but phrases do sound great when your ear has a few moments to digest them.

Another trick for holding your audience's ear is to repeat a phrase. "Solo Blue" repeats the first two bars in measures 5 and 6. This repetition would sound fine on its own, but here the line is developed further in measure 7, with a short phrase that acts like a nice tag or afterthought to the original, repeated phrase.

It's a good idea to try and keep from simply running up and down the scale too much. This will make your solos sound more like a scale exercise than an actual solo! Throughout "Solo Blue" you'll notice some fairly large leaps (measures 2, 6, 9, and 11), but measure 10 contrasts these leaps with shorter, stepwise motion, moving back up to the D note on beat three before moving down again.

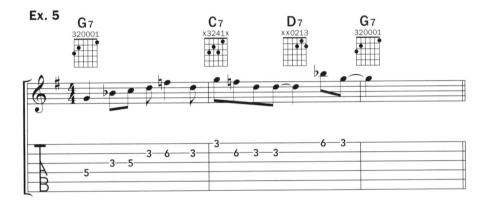

Solo Blue

Music by Andrew DuBrock

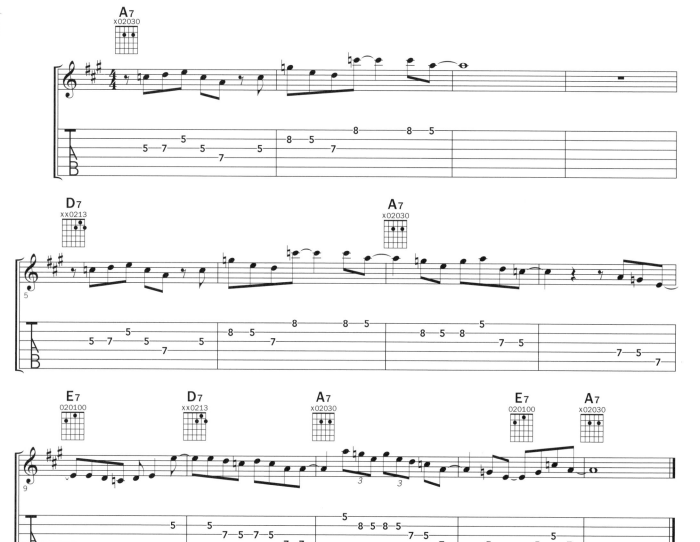

The Major-Pentatonic Scale

The major-pentatonic scale (**Example 6**) is built from the root, second, third, fifth, and sixth degrees and has a "happier" sound than the minor-pentatonic scale. Once you're familiar with the sound, try the extended C-major-pentatonic scale shown in **Example 7**. Unlike the minor-pentatonic pattern, this pattern starts one note *below* the root but ends on a root note at the very top.

Did you notice anything else about this scale? It's *exactly the same pattern* as the A-minor-pentatonic scale in Example 2! All major-pentatonic scales have a related minor-pentatonic scale three frets lower. When you play this pattern anywhere on the fretboard, the first note of the scale is your reference point. So, if you start the pattern with your index finger, you'll be playing a minor-pentatonic scale in the key of the note played by your index finger (in this case A minor). And if you start the scale with your pinky, you'll be playing a major-pentatonic scale in the key of the note played by your pinky (in this case C major).

While these patterns are the same, the minor-pentatonic and major pentatonic-scales for a given key sound quite different. Let's play a C-major-pentatonic and a C-minor-pentatonic scale to hear the difference. **Example 8** shows the C-major-pentatonic scale starting with your pinky on the root at the eighth fret. And **Example 9** shows the C-minor pentatonic scale starting with your index finger on the root at the eighth fret (check your fretting-hand fingering with the notation in examples 8 and 9 to be sure you're playing the shapes as efficiently as you can). You can hear that the scales are different, even though we're using the same basic shape. That's because the note relationships within the shape change because the root is in a different place within the pattern. So, once you know the movable shape, it's useful to know the relationship between the two scales, and that you can use the same shape to play both scales by starting in a different place. (Remember: starting with your index finger creates a minor-pentatonic scale while starting with your pinky creates a major-pentatonic scale.)

The major pentatonic is mostly used in a major context, and you often hear it in southern rock or country music. **Example 10** shows a major-pentatonic lick played over a C-major progression. As with minor-pentatonic scales, you can move your licks to play in any key. If someone's playing in D major, for example, simply slide the movable pattern up two frets so your pinky plays a D note on the sixth string (**Example 11**). For more on this, see "Building Pentatonic Scales in Any Key" on page 66.

Building a Major-Pentatonic Solo

Now let's try a solo using the major-pentatonic scale. "Sky-Blue Solo" (on page 67) uses many of the tricks you learned in the minor-pentatonic scale, but this time they're applied to the major-pentatonic scale. Rests and held notes in measures 2, 4, 8, 12–13, and 15 add a little of that breath-like quality to the solo.

In "Solo Blue" the first phrase is repeated verbatim, but "Sky-Blue Solo" takes this concept one step further: the *rhythms* and movement of the melody in certain phrases or partial phrases are repeated with different notes—a technique often called *sequencing*. To see how this works, look at the pattern of eighth notes that starts midway through measure 2 and ends on the C note in the middle of measure 3. Then compare this to the next set of eighth notes that starts in the second half of measure 3 and moves into the middle of measure 4. Notice that the rhythms are identical and the contour of the melody is also similar: both phrases move up or down the scale in the same way. This technique is also used in measures 5–6 and 9–10.

Now that you have a few tricks up your sleeve, you can start crafting your own solos with the minor- and major-pentatonic scales. At first, it may take awhile to come up with melodies you like, but once you're comfortable with these scales, the lines will come so quickly you'll be able to improvise interesting melodies on the fly!

Ex. 6: C-Major Pentatonic Scale   **Ex. 7: Extended C-Major Pentatonic Scale**

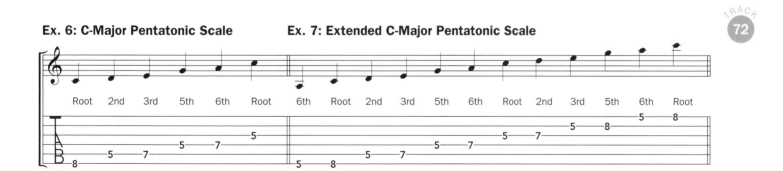

Ex. 8: C-Major Pentatonic Scale   **Ex. 9: C-Minor Pentatonic Scale**

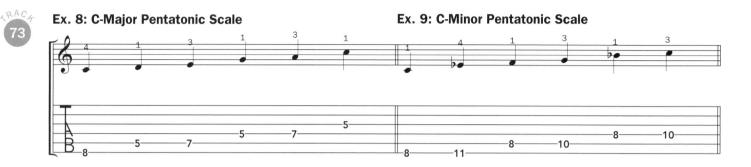

Ex. 10   **Ex. 11**

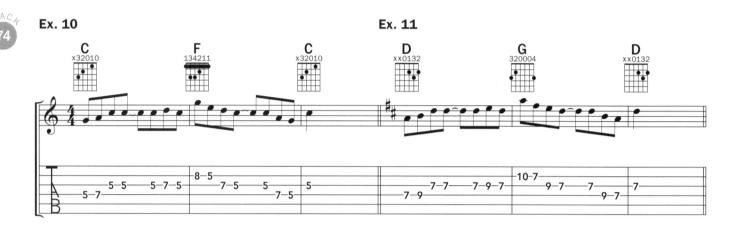

Building Pentatonic Scales in Any Key

Once your fingers have memorized the movable minor- and major-pentatonic scale shapes, you can slide them around the fretboard to play in any key. Here are the two shapes, with the root notes of each shape shown in circled dots:

 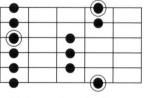

Minor-pentatonic shape   Major-pentatonic shape

To find the scales in specific keys, all you have to do is find the root note of the key you want to play on the sixth string, then place either your index (minor pentatonic) or pinky (major pentatonic) on that note to begin to play the appropriate movable shape. For instance, if you want to play a B♭-minor-pentatonic scale, find B♭ on the sixth string, place your index finger on that fret and play the minor-pentatonic shape. If you want to play a C-major-pentatonic scale, find the C note on the sixth string, place your pinky on that fret, and play through the major-pentatonic shape. Here are the notes on the sixth string, to help you get going:

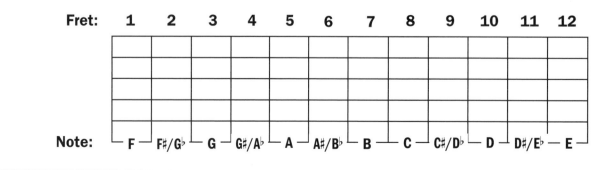

Fret:	1	2	3	4	5	6	7	8	9	10	11	12
Note:	F	F♯/G♭	G	G♯/A♭	A	A♯/B♭	B	C	C♯/D♭	D	D♯/E♭	E

Sky-Blue Solo

Music by Andrew DuBrock

Play Leads with Major and Minor Scales

Listen to any guitar solo in your music collection—like the ones in the Beatles' "And Your Bird Can Sing" or the Allman Brothers Band's "Jessica"—and it's a good bet that it uses notes from a major scale. That's because the major scale is the foundation of Western music. And I don't mean "country" music. I'm talking about the music of Western civilization! Many guitar leads are built exclusively from the major scale, and almost everything else in Western music is based around variations on the major scale. For example, the next most important scale—the minor scale—is based on the major scale, and is another major source for rock guitar leads. So let's look at how the major and minor scales are constructed and related and play a few leads with these two blockbusters. We'll start with the granddaddy: the major scale.

The Major Scale

First, let's look at the anatomy of the major scale, because once you understand how that is put together, you'll be on the road to soloing like your favorite guitarists. **Example 1** shows the seven notes that make up the major scale—in this case, a G-major scale. If you've explored the Soloing with Pentatonic Scales lesson,

you'll notice that the major scale encompasses the major pentatonic and adds two more notes: the fourth and seventh of the key. Like pentatonic scales, the patterns that make up major and minor scales can be found and repeated all over the fretboard. The starting note of the scale, in this case, G, is called the *root* and once you cycle through all seven notes of the scale, it repeats—the eighth note of the scale is another root note.

Scales are made up of *half steps* (the distance of one fret) and *whole steps* (two frets) and are built by combining half steps and whole steps in a specific order. As you can see in Example 1, in a major scale these steps fall in the following order: whole, whole, half, whole, whole, whole, half. You can use this configuration to build a major scale starting on any note. Let's try C, down at the third fret. If you move up using the whole- and half-step major-scale formula, you get **Example 2**, a C-major scale.

Now let's go back to the G-major scale. If you move up to the seventh position, with your index finger at the seventh fret, you can cycle through the G-major scale more than once by starting on the third below the root and continuing up to the high fifth on the first string (**Example 3**).

TRACK 76

Ex. 1: G-Major Scale

Ex. 2: C-Major Scale

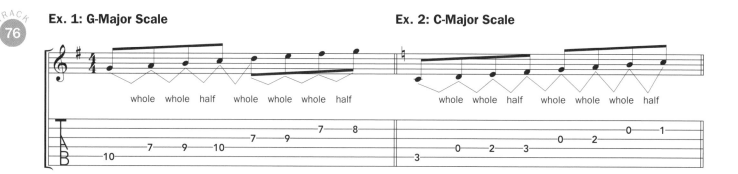

TRACK 77

Ex. 3: Extended G-Major Scale

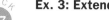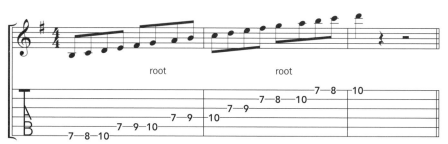

Practice the scale a few times, and then try **Example 4**, which shows the melody to the traditional hymn "Simple Gifts" played using the major scale. **Example 5** shows a major-scale lead similar to Dickey Betts's solo on the Allman Brothers Band's "Jessica." Since this is a closed-position scale shape (there are no open strings), you can transfer it to any other key, just like we did with the major and minor pentatonic scales in previous lessons. Do this by finding the root note on the fifth string and using the same basic major-scale patterns we used with the G-major scale. **Example 6** shows this lead transposed down a whole step (two frets) to the key of F major.

Unlocking the Scale Formula

So what happens when you want to play a melody that extends below or above the scale position you just learned? Let's say you want to play Example 5 down one *octave* (an octave is the distance from one root to the next). The fretboard is filled with interlocking major-scale patterns, and you can use the major-scale formula to find single-octave and extended major scales *anywhere* on the fretboard. Since we know that the lowest note in Example 5 is the root note of the scale (G), let's find a G note down an octave and build a G-major scale starting from there. There's a G note at the third fret of the sixth string, so start with

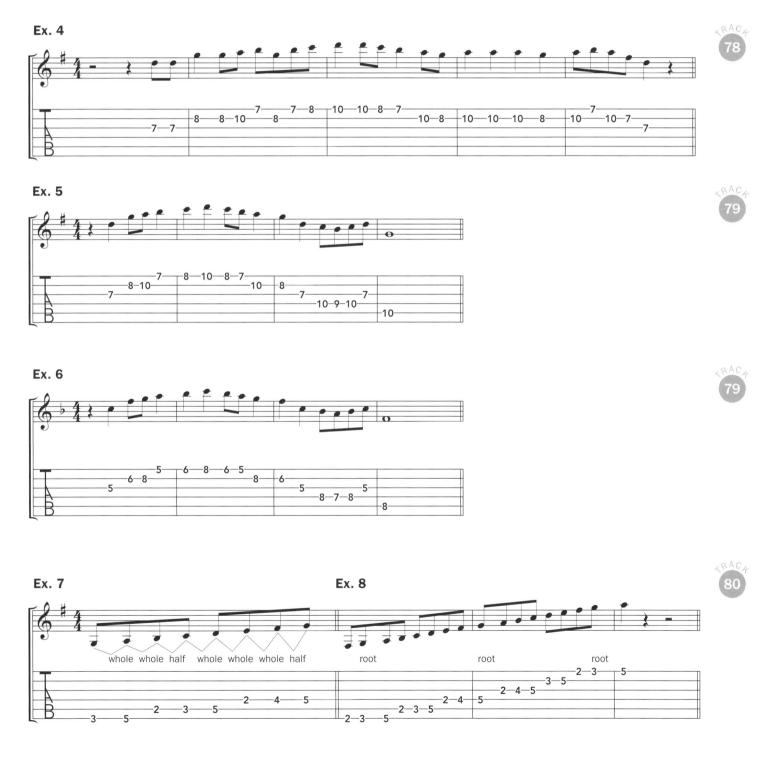

your middle finger and build a major scale using the whole- and half-step formula (**Example 7**). You can also play more than one octave in this position. **Example 8** shows how far we can get if we extend the scale down (just one note) and all the way up to the first string—a scale spanning over two octaves. You can also play the melody from Example 5 in its original key of G, but down one octave (**Example 9**).

Now that you have two extended major-scale shapes that work in different areas of the fretboard, you can play almost any melody in any key. Whatever key you're in, your hands will be close to *one* of these shapes. Just find the closest root note on the fifth or sixth string and play the appropriate pattern. Of course, since you know the major-scale formula, you can also find other

places to play the major scale (see "Building Major and Minor Scales Anywhere in Any Key," on page 74, to explore this further).

Building a Major-Scale Solo

Let's finish our major-scale study by playing through a complete tune. "Sunnyside Solo" uses the G-major scale to craft a solo over a pop-rock chord progression in G. The lead starts with a fairly constant stream of eighth notes, but solos can sound like just a barrage of notes if they don't pause to "breathe" like a singer does. That's exactly what happens in measure 4, with the held half note. Repeated patterns can also make a solo interesting, and you'll find this in the rhythmic pattern in which a half note is followed by three eighth notes in measures 7, 8, and 10.

Ex. 9

Sunnyside Solo

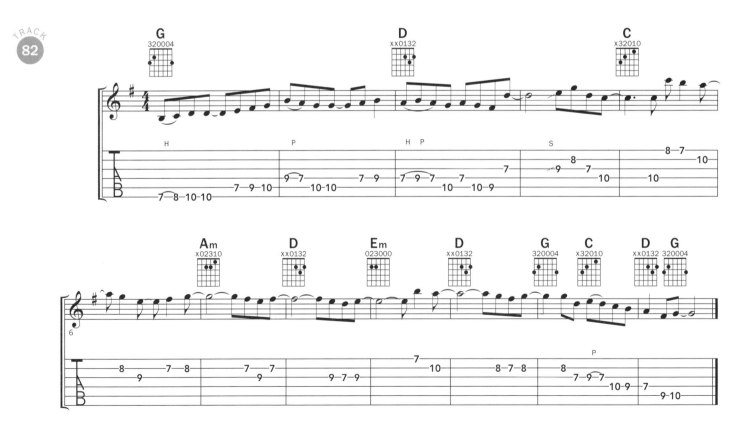

The Minor Scale

Now let's compare the major scale with the second-most popular scale in Western music, the minor scale. Play through the E-minor scale shown in **Example 10**. If these notes seem familiar that's because you've already played these shapes in the extended G-major scale in Example 3. These two scales share the same notes. Because of this, we call E minor the *relative minor* of G major (and G the *relative major* of Em). **Example 11** highlights this relationship so that you can see it more clearly. The relative-minor scale is built from the sixth degree of the corresponding major scale. So if you count up (or down) to the sixth degree of any major scale, you'll find the root note of its relative-minor scale. Likewise, if you count up (or down) to the third degree of any minor scale, you'll be at the root note of its relative-major scale.

Of course, these scales sound very different because—though they share the same notes—they start and end in different places.

Play through the major-scale examples, and notice how this scale sounds "happy." Now play through the minor scale, and you'll see why it's often described as a sad-sounding scale. The difference in sound is due to the order of steps in the scales. The order of steps in the minor-scale is whole, half, whole, whole, half, whole, whole. You can build any minor scale by starting on a pitch and applying this formula as you add notes. **Example 12** shows the A-minor scale.

Now let's move back to the E-minor scale and play through its extended version in the seventh position (**Example 13**). In this position, the scale extends down to the lower fifth (B) and up to the seventh (D). Experiment with this scale to come up with your own phrases, like the one in **Example 14**. Just as with the major scale, you can transfer this minor-scale shape to any other key. **Example 15** slides the phrase from Example 11 up one fret to the key of F minor.

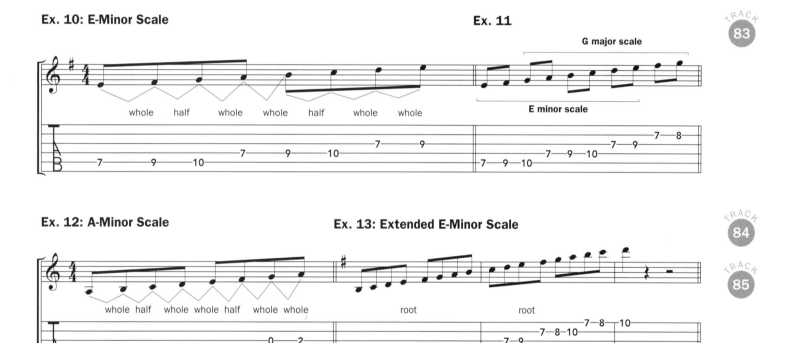

Ex. 10: E-Minor Scale

Ex. 11

TRACK 83

Ex. 12: A-Minor Scale

Ex. 13: Extended E-Minor Scale

TRACK 84

TRACK 85

Since you know that major and minor scales share the same shapes, it will be clear that we can use the second extended major-scale shape from Example 8 as another minor-scale pattern to play melodies in a different part of the neck. The minor scale uses the same pattern as the major scale, but it starts in a different place. **Example 16** shows where the root notes fall when using this shape for an E-minor scale. Now let's try the phrase from Example 15 down an octave using this pattern (**Example 17**). As with the major scale, whatever minor key you're in, your hands will be close to *one* of these shapes. Just find the closest root note on the fifth or sixth string and play the appropriate pattern. Of course, since you know the minor-scale formula, you can also find other places to play the minor scale (see "Building Major and Minor Scales Anywhere in Any Key" on page 74).

Building a Minor-Scale Solo

Now let's try a solo using the minor scale. "Full Moon Solo" uses the classic chord progression that Led Zeppelin used behind possibly the greatest solo of all time: "Stairway to Heaven." In the key of E minor, the progression moves from Em through D to C. Notice the rhythmic repetition in measures 5–7, and watch out for the *grace notes*—those small notes with lines through the top. To play these notes, fret the small note, pluck the string on the beat, then quickly hammer-on to the next note. At the end of the solo, the chord progression moves down through Am for a smoother resolution to Em.

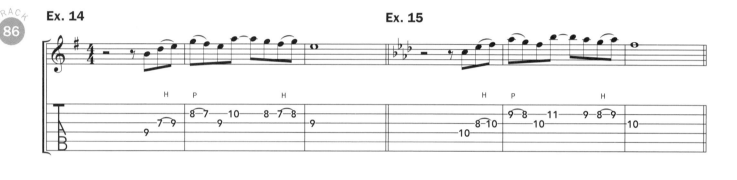

Ex. 14   Ex. 15

TRACK 86

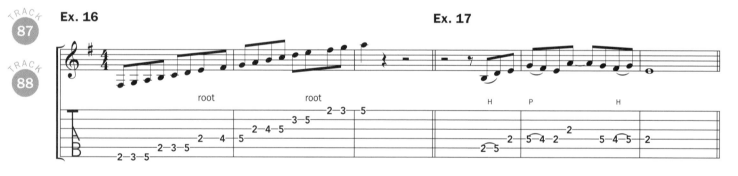

Ex. 16   Ex. 17

TRACK 87

TRACK 88

Full Moon Solo

Music by Andrew DuBrock

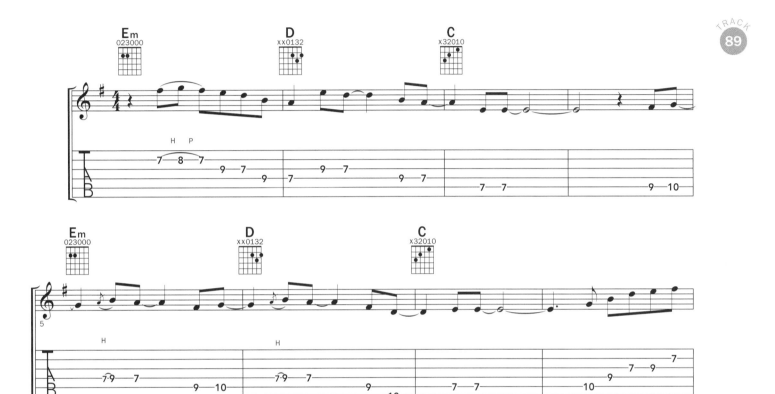

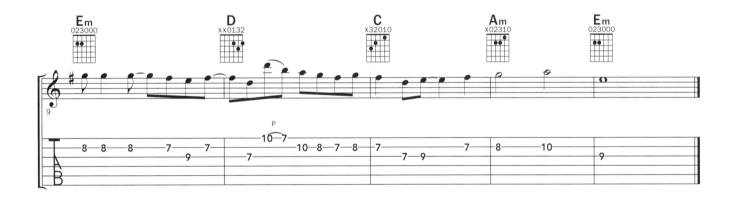

Building Major or Minor Scales Anywhere in Any Key

Once your fingers have memorized the two movable major- and minor-scale shapes learned in this lesson, you can slide them around the fretboard to play in any key. Here are the shapes—used for both major and minor scales—with their respective root notes circled.

To find the scales in specific keys, all you have to do is find the root note of the key you want to play on the fourth, fifth, or sixth string, then place the appropriate finger (depending on the pattern you're using) on that note to start playing the matching movable scale shape. For instance, if you want to play a B♭-major scale, find B♭ on the sixth string, place your middle finger on that fret and play major-scale shape 2. You could also find B♭ on the fifth string, which is way up at the 13th fret! (The B♭ on the first fret is too low to use either of these patterns.) Place your pinky on that fret and play through major-scale shape 1. If you want to play a B♭-*minor* scale, find the B♭ note on the fifth string, place your index finger on that fret, and play through minor-scale shape 1. To use minor-scale shape 2, find the B♭ note on the fourth string, place your index finger on that fret, and play through the shape. Here are the notes on the fourth, fifth, and sixth strings, to help you get going:

But what if you want to play a minor scale that starts with a note on the sixth string? The magic of the major- and minor-scale formulas is that we can create these scales starting *anywhere*—we simply find a new shape for the scale that we didn't already know. For example, to find a B♭-minor scale that starts on the sixth string first find the

B♭ note at the sixth fret. Then, apply the half- and whole-step formula to build a B♭-minor scale. **Example 18** shows how this looks when you start with your index finger. But you can also start with another finger, like your pinky, as shown in **Example 19**, which is *another* minor-scale shape! Try this out on your own—for both major- and minor-scale shapes. Over time, you'll discover patterns that span the entire fretboard, and eventually you'll be able to move between all of these patterns to play any scale anywhere on the neck of your guitar.

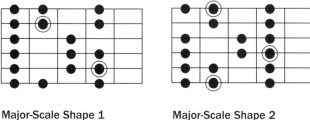

Major-Scale Shape 1   Major-Scale Shape 2

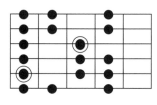 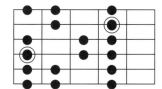

Minor-Scale Shape 1   Minor-Scale Shape 2

Fret:	1	2	3	4	5	6	7	8	9	10	11	12
Notes:	D♯/E♭	E	F	F♯/G♭	G	G♯/A♭	A	A♯/B♭	B	C	C♯/D♭	D
	A♯/B♭	B	C	C♯/D♭	D	D♯/E♭	E	F	F♯/G♭	G	G♯/A♭	A
	F	F♯/G♭	G	G♯/A♭	A	A♯/B♭	B	C	C♯/D♭	D	D♯/E♭	E

Ex. 18

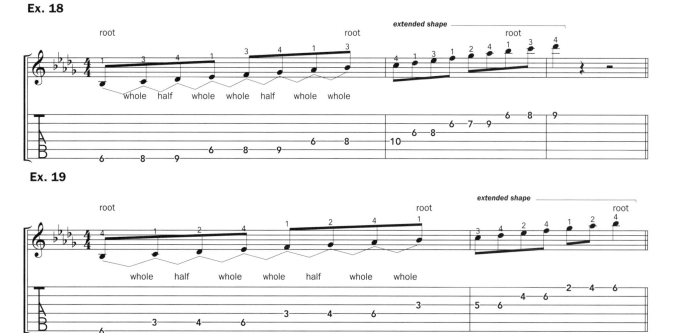

Ex. 19

Play Leads with Arpeggios

Most guitarists start playing leads by learning how to play scales, and this is a great way to begin, but scales are just one way to play solo lines. Scales move from note to note in a stepwise manner—like walking up and down stairs one at a time. This works, of course, but it can be more interesting when you skip a step or two every so often. One way of skipping notes in scales is by playing *arpeggios*. Think about the anthemic, fading melody line in the Eagles "Hotel California," the climax to the solo in the Dire Straits song "Sultans of Swing," or the melody in the Allman Brothers song "Jessica." These are all arpeggios. In this lesson, you'll learn what an arpeggio is, how to find arpeggios that work in solos over any chord, and how to integrate arpeggios into your lead lines, making your solos and melodies sound more varied, interesting, and fluid.

All About Arpeggios

When you break a chord up into its individual notes, you're playing an arpeggio. Take a first-position E chord and play the individual notes from the sixth string up to the first string and back down, as shown in **Example 1**, and you're arpeggiating an E chord. Playing chords as arpeggios works great as an alternative backup pattern to strumming. Try this the next time you're playing rhythm—especially when there is more than one guitar playing the chords. In Example 1 each note of the E chord is played in sequence, but you can jump around, playing the notes in any order, as in **Example 2**. You can arpeggiate six-string chord shapes like these, but to play every possible note in an arpeggio, you'll need to play a few more notes. That's because a full six-string chord shape like this doesn't include every possible root, third, and fifth of the chord—the notes you use to build a major chord. **Example 3** shows an E arpeggio that includes all possible notes in the first position.

Bite-Size Arpeggio Shapes

As Examples 1–3 show, arpeggios can stretch all the way across the fretboard, but they can also be broken up into smaller, three- or four-note patterns that you can easily move to fit any progression or song. We'll focus on small, three-note arpeggio shapes on the top four strings because they are easy to visualize and piece together, they're big enough to enhance a song, and they're all you need to make great sounding leads. Over time, you'll see how the shapes all fit together, and you'll eventually see virtual arpeggio maps all over the fretboard.

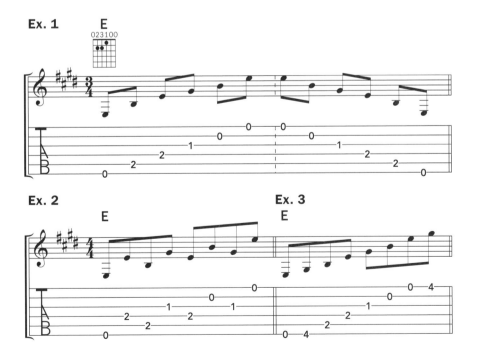

First, let's look at the three-note groups we can get from an E chord on the top four strings. Look back at Example 3 and you can see the three possibilities shown in **Example 4**. We're just using descending arpeggios here, instead of the ascending arpeggios in Example 3. All three of these shapes include the root, third, and fifth of the E chord. Some other notes will work, but in this lesson we'll use arpeggio shapes that have the root, third, and fifth because these are the notes that major and minor chords are built from, and all of the chord progressions we'll play over will use major and minor chords.

You can move the patterns up the fretboard by translating these three bite-size arpeggios into movable shapes. Play arpeggios using the shapes in **Example 5** at the first fret, and you're playing F arpeggios. Play them at the third fret, and you're playing G arpeggios, and so on. To help you get your bearings, I've circled the root note in each arpeggio.

Now let's apply this arpeggio pattern to a chord progression, moving the middle shape around over a C–G–B♭–F chord progression (**Example 6**). Notice that we change the arpeggio shape to match the background chord—over a C chord, we play a C arpeggio (with the root note at the eighth fret), and so on.

Interlocking Patterns of Arpeggios

Example 6 sounds pretty good, but you have to jump all over the place to grab each chord. We can solve this by using other chord shapes to build arpeggios. Let's look at a C arpeggio now. **Example 7** shows a C-chord arpeggio and a full C arpeggio at the nut. **Example 8** shows the three-note arpeggios and movable three-note shapes we can get from this full C arpeggio. When you play these shapes at the first fret you get a D♭ arpeggio, play them at the second fret and you get a D arpeggio, etc. (In fact, you'll notice that the second movable arpeggio shape in Example 8 looks just like a first-position D chord.)

Now, let's integrate this shape into the C–G–B♭–F chord progression by playing it over the G and F chords (**Example 9**). Notice that you don't have to jump around the fretboard like you did in Example 8—the arpeggio shapes interlock. At this point, you're playing leads like Joe Walsh did at the very end of the Eagles "Hotel California" (the repeating line that fades out). Try plugging in the first shape from the E- and C-shape arpeggios for the chords in **Example 10**, add some pull-offs, and you're playing leads like Mark Knopfler did in the scorching climax to his solo on "Sultans of Swing."

TRACK 91

Ex. 4
Three-note E arpeggio shapes:

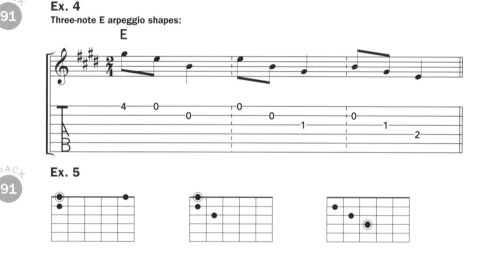

TRACK 91

Ex. 5

TRACK 92

Ex. 6

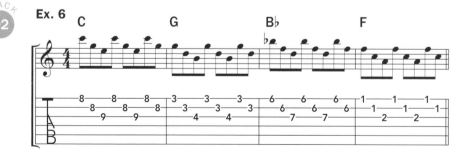

Ex. 7
C chord arpeggio: Extended C arpeggio:

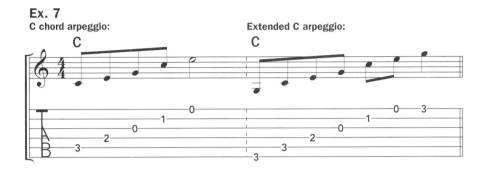

Ex. 8
Three-note C arpeggio shapes:

Moveable arpeggio shapes:

Ex. 9

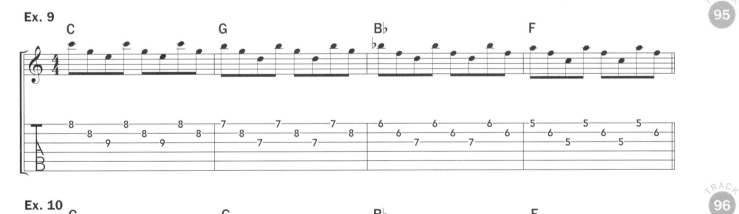

Ex. 10

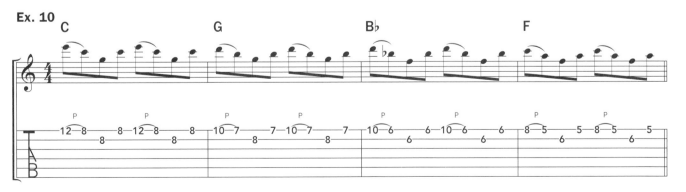

So far, we've only built arpeggios from two basic chord shapes, but we already have a set of shapes that will interlock all over the fretboard. Let's try building arpeggios from one more chord shape—an A shape. **Example 11** shows an arpeggiated A chord alongside an extended A arpeggio in root position, and **Example 12** shows the three-note A arpeggios and the movable three-note shapes we can get from our A shape.

Now let's try using these arpeggio shapes in the C–G–B♭–F chord progression. If we play the first two measures like we did in Example 11, we can slide the C-shape arpeggio up to play B♭ arpeggios, putting us in perfect position to use the A-shape arpeggio over the F chord (**Example 13**). And you can also play the same progression using the arpeggios we've already learned on the guitar's middle strings, as in **Example 14**.

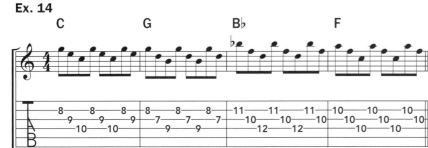

Integrate Arpeggio Shapes into Your Leads

While arpeggios sound great on their own for a short passage or several measures of a solo, arpeggiated sections stand out even more when they have something to contrast with. Now that you have the shapes under your fingers, let's integrate arpeggios into a complete lead melody: "Arpeggio Annie." With ideas similar to the Allman Brothers' song "Jessica," "Arpeggio Annie" combines arpeggios with stepwise scale motion for a bouncy, acoustic rocker. I've highlighted the arpeggios throughout the notation with the abbreviation "arp" so you can quickly see where each one occurs. Note how the arpeggios are sandwiched between scale lines in the A section, but are fairly spread out in the B section. This is done so that the B section as a whole contrasts with the A section. Having fewer arpeggios makes your ear ready again for the arpeggio-saturated A section that follows. While most of the arpeggios are three-note groups, a few of them use only two notes—such as the D arpeggio in measure 15. And in measure 25, the A arpeggio skips the middle note in the three-note shape. Also check out the move in measure 33, where two three-note shapes in a row create a longer arpeggio—the open E string is used as a transition to give your hand time to shift up to the higher shape.

"Arpeggio Annie" begs to be played at a brisk tempo, but slow it down considerably while you practice it. Once you can comfortably play it cleanly at a very slow tempo, gradually increase the speed until you can play it cleanly at performance tempo. The A section stays high up the neck in the same general vicinity, but a long set of slides down the fretboard brings you down to the nut of the guitar in the B section. Try following the suggested fingerings throughout before coming up with your own way of playing the song.

Arpeggios for Any Chord

We've exclusively used major-chord arpeggios throughout this lesson, but you can create and use arpeggios for any chord type by applying these same methods to any chord type you want—whether it's an Am, Csus2, or Bm7♭5! Simply apply the arpeggio concept to whatever chord shape you're playing, by picking the notes of the chord individually. For instance, here are three ways you can arpeggiate a Cadd9 chord at the nut of the guitar (**Example A**). Find your own arpeggio patterns and try them out with any chord shape in your repertoire.

Ex. A

Arpeggio pattern 1:   Arpeggio pattern 2:   Arpeggio pattern 3:

Arpeggio Annie

Words and music by Andrew DuBrock

TRACK 99

Played with a full band,
then played without the band.

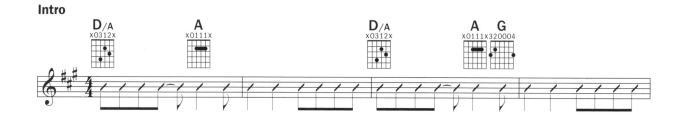

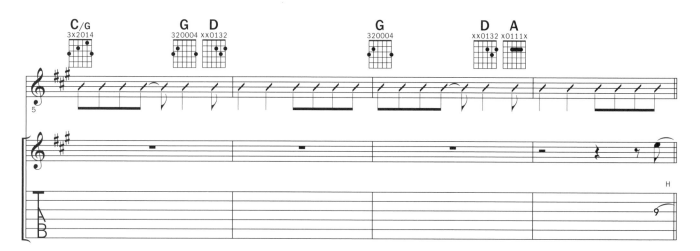

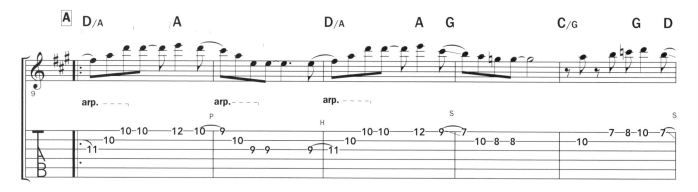

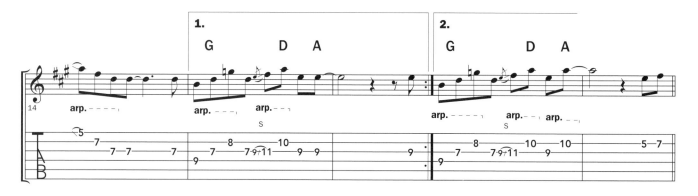

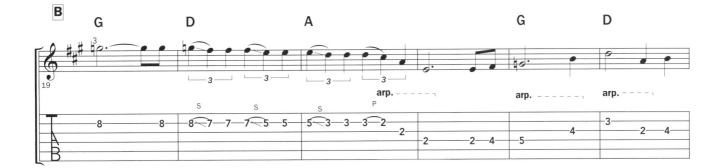

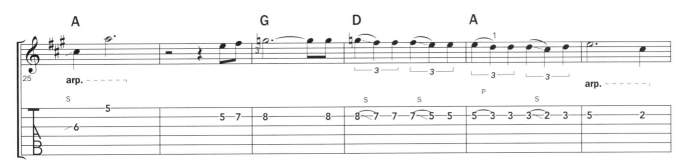

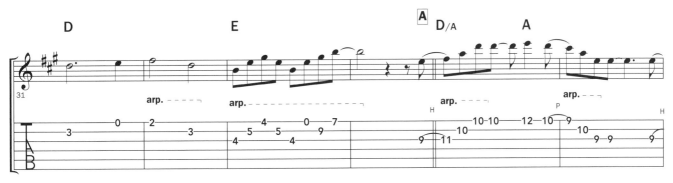

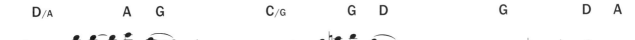

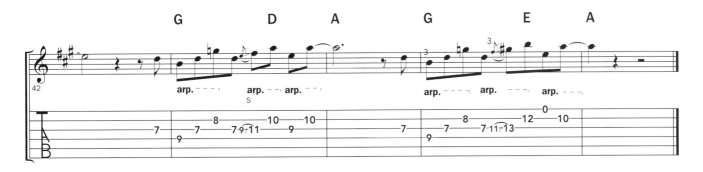

About the Author

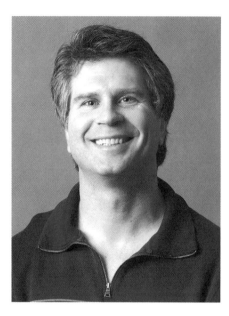

Andrew DuBrock, a contributing editor to *Acoustic Guitar*, writes instructional books and articles, and transcribes, edits, and engraves music for print and multimedia publications, including *Acoustic Guitar*, Homespun, Hal Leonard, Alfred, and independent musicians like Alex de Grassi and Michelle Shocked.

DuBrock, who was *Acoustic Guitar*'s music editor from 1999–2007, is also the author of *Total Acoustic Guitar* (Hal Leonard) and the video instructor and author of *The Guitarist's Personal Practice Trainer* (Homespun). While he predominately writes guitar instructional materials, he was initially trained as a classical pianist and honed his musical skills by playing French horn in symphonies and singing baritone in choral groups. He received a BA in music from Brown University. He writes and records music as a singer-songwriter, and his self-produced album can be found at amazon.com under the group name "DuBrock".

To see more books and articles by DuBrock, or leave a comment or ask questions about this book, visit andrewdubrock.com.

GUITAR LEARNING HAS GONE MOBILE

Acoustic Guitar U—The Next Level in Guitar Learning

No music book? No music stand? No sheet music? NO PROBLEM.

Log onto **AcousticGuitarU.com** from your PC, laptop, tablet, or smartphone and check out our ever-growing library of online guitar lessons, complete courses, and songs to learn. Enjoy:

- **Best-of-the-web audio and video instruction in a wide variety of styles and topics**

- **Easy-to-follow lessons for all levels from total beginner to advanced**

- **Streaming content, which means no more time spent waiting for files to download**

Learn acoustic guitar anytime, anywhere. All you need is access to the internet.

MORE TITLES FROM STRINGLETTER

Learn authentic techniques, hone your skills, and expand your understanding of musical essentials with the help of our song and lesson books including:

Explore Alternate Tunings

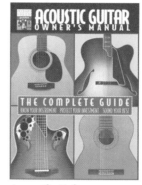

Acoustic Guitar Owner's Manual

Acoustic Blues Guitar Essentials

Classical Guitar Answer Book

The Acoustic Guitar Method Complete Edition

Songwriting and the Guitar

Become a better guitarist and more informed instrument owner with our range of informative guides. *Acoustic Guitar Guides* offer video and written instruction and can be downloaded as individual lessons, or complete courses. Popular titles include:

Acoustic Guitar Amplification Essentials: Complete Edition
Get answers to all your acoustic amplification questions with this complete guide series featuring both video and written instruction. Learn how to use monitors, PAs, EQ, and effects; discover the differences between the various pickups and how to install them, and learn how to choose and position microphones to capture your guitar's natural tone. *By Doug Young.*

Acoustic Guitar Slide Basics: Complete Edition
Master one of the great styles of American roots music with the help of these nine progressive lessons (video and written instruction) on the fundamentals of acoustic slide guitar. *By David Hamburger.*

Acoustic Blues Guitar Basics: Fingerstyle Blues
Learn basic fingerpicking blues patterns played by blues greats like Reverend Gary Davis and Robert Johnson. Try Piedmont and Delta fingerpicking styles, and play two complete 12-bar fingerstyle tunes. *By Orville Johnson.*

Visit **Store.AcousticGuitar.com** today for the full range of Acoustic Guitar products.